COUNTRY CASSEROLES

DEBBIE MUMM.

D0047979

pil

Publications International, Ltd.

Favorite Brand Name Recipes at www.fbnr.com

Microwave Cooking: Microwave ovens vary in wattage. Use the cooking times as guidelines and check for doneness before adding more time.

Preparation/Cooking Times: Preparation times are based on the approximate amount of time required to assemble the recipe before cooking, baking, chilling or serving. These times include preparation steps such as measuring, chopping and mixing. The fact that some preparations and cooking can be done simultaneously is taken into account. Preparation of optional ingredients and serving suggestions is not included.

Contents

Breakfast Casserole

6 large eggs, beaten
½ cup sour cream
1 can (15 ounces) VEG•ALL® Original Mixed
    Vegetables, drained
1 cup frozen cubed hash brown potatoes, thawed
1 cup smoked sausage links, chopped
1 cup shredded pepper-jack cheese
2 tablespoons canned jalapeño pepper slices
1 cup broken tortilla chips

Preheat oven to 350°F.

In medium bowl, combine eggs and sour cream until smooth. Fold in remaining ingredients except tortilla chips.

Transfer mixture to greased 11×7-inch baking dish. Bake for 25 to 30 minutes or until eggs are set and puffed.

Top with tortilla chips and bake an additional 5 minutes. Serve with additional sour cream on the side, if desired.

Serve with fresh fruit for breakfast or brunch.

Makes 6 to 8 servings

Tip: For a milder flavor, substitute chopped fresh cilantro for the sliced jalapeño peppers.

Baked French Toast Wedges

    4 whole BAYS® English muffins, cut into 1-inch cubes
    3 large eggs
    ½ cup sugar
    1 teaspoon cinnamon
    1 teaspoon vanilla
    ¼ teaspoon salt
1⅔ cups half-and-half, whipping cream or whole milk
    2 tablespoons butter or margarine, melted
    ⅛ teaspoon nutmeg, preferably freshly grated
    Fruit topping (optional)

Spray 10-inch quiche dish or deep-dish pie plate with nonstick cooking spray. Arrange muffins in single layer in dish. In medium bowl, beat together eggs and combined sugar and cinnamon. Stir in vanilla and salt; mix well. Add half-and-half and melted butter, mixing well. Pour evenly over muffins; press down on muffins to moisten with liquid. Sprinkle evenly with nutmeg. Cover and refrigerate overnight, if desired, or bake immediately.

Bake in 350°F oven for 40 to 45 minutes or until puffed and golden brown. Transfer to cooling rack; cool at least 10 minutes before serving.* Cut into wedges and serve warm with desired fruit topping or heated maple syrup.   *Makes 6 servings*

At this point, French toast may be cooled completely, cut into wedges, placed between sheets of waxed paper in a plastic freezer storage bag and frozen up to 1 month. Place wedges on baking sheet and bake in 350°F oven for 8 to 10 minutes or until thawed and heated through.

Mixed Fruit Topping: Combine 1 peeled and diced kiwifruit, ½ cup fresh raspberries and 1 sliced ripe small banana with 2 tablespoons honey and 2 teaspoons fresh lime juice. Let stand 5 minutes.

Strawberry Topping: Combine 1¼ cups thinly sliced strawberries, ¼ cup strawberry jam or currant jelly and 1 teaspoon orange juice** in microwave-safe bowl. Cover and cook at High power 1 minute or until warm. (Or, heat in small saucepan over medium heat until warm.) **Almond or orange-flavored liqueur may be substituted, if desired.

6

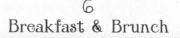

Breakfast & Brunch

Peachy Keen Topping: Combine ¼ cup peach or apricot preserves and 1 tablespoon pineapple or apple juice.*** Add 1 peeled and diced ripe peach or 1 cup diced thawed frozen sliced peaches, ¼ cup fresh or partially thawed frozen blueberries, mixing well. Serve at room temperature or heat as for Strawberry Topping above. ***Almond or orange-flavored liqueur may be substituted, if desired.

Baked Ham & Cheese Monte Cristo

   6 slices bread, divided
   2 cups (8 ounces) shredded Cheddar cheese, divided
   1⅓ cups *French's*® French Fried Onions, divided
   1 package (10 ounces) frozen broccoli spears, thawed,
       drained and cut into 1-inch pieces
   2 cups (10 ounces) cubed cooked ham
   5 eggs
   2 cups milk
   ½ teaspoon ground mustard
   ½ teaspoon seasoned salt
   ¼ teaspoon coarsely ground black pepper

Preheat oven to 325°F. Cut 3 bread slices into cubes; place in greased 12×8-inch baking dish. Top bread with 1 cup cheese, ⅔ *cup* French Fried Onions, broccoli and ham. Cut remaining bread slices diagonally into halves. Arrange bread halves down center of casserole, overlapping slightly, crusted points all in one direction.

In medium bowl, beat eggs, milk and seasonings; pour evenly over casserole. Bake, uncovered, at 325°F for 1 hour or until center is set. Top with remaining 1 cup cheese and ⅔ *cup* onions; bake, uncovered, 5 minutes or until onions are golden brown. Let stand 10 minutes before serving. *Makes 6 to 8 servings*

Lit'l Links Soufflé

8 slices white bread
2 cups (8 ounces) shredded Cheddar cheese
1 pound HILLSHIRE FARM® Lit'l Polskas
6 eggs
2¾ cups milk
¾ teaspoon dry mustard

Arrange bread in bottom of greased 13×9-inch baking pan. Sprinkle cheese over top of bread.

Arrange Lit'l Polskas on top of cheese. Beat eggs with milk and mustard in large bowl; pour over links. Cover pan with aluminum foil; refrigerate overnight.

Preheat oven to 300°F. Bake egg mixture 1½ hours or until puffy and brown. *Makes 4 to 6 servings*

Potato Bacon Casserole

4 cups frozen shredded hash brown potatoes
½ cup finely chopped onion
8 ounces bacon or turkey bacon, cooked and crumbled*
1 cup (4 ounces) shredded cheddar cheese
1 can (12 fluid ounces) NESTLÉ® CARNATION® Evaporated Milk or NESTLÉ® CARNATION® Evaporated Lowfat Milk
1 large egg, lightly beaten or ¼ cup egg substitute
1½ teaspoons seasoned salt

Can substitute with 1 package (2.1 ounces) precooked bacon slices, cut into small pieces.

PREHEAT oven to 350°F. Grease 8-inch square baking dish.

LAYER ½ potatoes, ½ onion, ½ bacon and ½ cheese in prepared baking dish; repeat layers. Combine evaporated milk, egg and seasoned salt in small bowl. Pour evenly over potato mixture; cover.

BAKE for 55 to 60 minutes. Uncover; bake for an additional 5 minutes. Let stand for 10 to 15 minutes before serving. *Makes 6 servings*

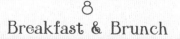

Breakfast & Brunch

Bacon and Maple Grits Puff

8 slices bacon
2 cups milk
1¼ cups water
1 cup uncooked quick-cooking grits
½ teaspoon salt
½ cup pure maple syrup
4 eggs
Fresh chives (optional)

1. Preheat oven to 350°F. Grease 1½-quart round casserole or soufflé dish; set aside.

2. Cook bacon in large skillet over medium-high heat about 7 minutes or until crisp. Remove bacon to paper towels; set aside. Reserve 2 tablespoons bacon drippings.

3. Combine milk, water, grits and salt in medium saucepan. Bring to a boil over medium heat, stirring frequently. Simmer 2 to 3 minutes or until mixture thickens, stirring constantly. Remove from heat; stir in syrup and reserved 2 tablespoons bacon drippings.

4. Crumble bacon; reserve ¼ cup for garnish. Stir remaining crumbled bacon into grits mixture.

5. Beat eggs in medium bowl. Gradually stir small amount of grits mixture into eggs. Stir egg mixture into remaining grits mixture. Pour into prepared casserole.

6. Bake 1 hour and 20 minutes or until knife inserted into center comes out clean. Top with reserved ¼ cup bacon. Garnish with fresh chives. Serve immediately. *Makes 6 to 8 servings*

Note: Puff will fall slightly after being removed from oven.

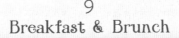

Breakfast & Brunch

Cheddar Oven Omelet

  4 large eggs
  2 tablespoons milk
  ⅛ teaspoon salt
  Pinch ground black pepper
  ¼ cup diced jarred roasted red peppers
  2 tablespoons chopped green onions
  **1 cup grated CABOT® Sharp, Extra Sharp or Hunter's
     Cheddar, divided**

1. Place rack in center of oven and preheat oven to 400°F. Coat pie plate or small shallow baking dish with nonstick cooking spray or brush with oil.

2. In medium bowl, whisk eggs until combined and frothy. Add milk, salt and black pepper; whisk again. Stir in roasted red peppers, green onions and ¾ cup cheese.

3. Pour mixture into prepared pie plate, distributing evenly. Bake for 12 to 15 minutes or until puffed and center is set. Remove from oven and sprinkle with remaining ¼ cup cheese.   *Makes 2 servings*

Biscuit and Sausage Bake

  2 cups biscuit baking mix
  ½ cup milk
  1 egg
  1 teaspoon vanilla
  1 cup fresh or frozen blueberries
  6 fully cooked breakfast sausage links, thawed if frozen
  Maple syrup, warmed

1. Preheat oven to 350° F. Spray 8-inch square pan with nonstick cooking spray. Whisk baking mix, milk, egg and vanilla in medium bowl. Stir in blueberries. (Batter will be stiff.) Spread batter into prepared pan.

2. Cut each sausage link into small pieces. Sprinkle sausage pieces over batter. Bake 22 minutes or until lightly browned on top. Cut into squares; serve with warm maple syrup.   *Makes 6 servings*

Smoked Cheese and Muffin Strata

        6 BAYS® English Muffins, cubed
        8 ounces smoked Gouda cheese, sliced
        8 ounces Cheddar cheese, sliced
        8 ounces pork or turkey bulk sausage, cooked and crumbled
    4¾ cups milk
        8 eggs
      ⅓ cup diced red pepper
      ⅓ cup diced green pepper
        1 teaspoon salt
          Pinch ground black pepper
          Paprika, to taste

Line bottom of 13×9-inch pan with half of muffin cubes. Arrange cheeses evenly over muffin cubes in pan. Sprinkle with crumbled sausage. Arrange remaining muffin cubes in pan over sausage and cheese layers.

Mix together milk, eggs, bell peppers, salt and black pepper. Pour over ingredients in pan. Press down on muffin cubes to soak thoroughly. Sprinkle with paprika. Cover with plastic wrap. Refrigerate 8 hours or overnight.

Bake, uncovered, in 325°F oven for just over 2 hours or until knife inserted near center comes out clean. Let stand 5 minutes before serving. *Makes 6 servings*

Note: Recipe may be halved. Bake in an 8-inch square pan for 1 hour and 15 minutes or until a knife inserted near the center comes out clean.

Hearty Breakfast Custard Casserole

1 pound (2 medium-large) Colorado baking potatoes
 Salt and black pepper
8 ounces low-fat bulk pork sausage, cooked and crumbled *or*
 6 ounces finely diced lean ham *or* **6 ounces turkey**
 bacon, cooked and crumbled
⅓ cup julienne-sliced roasted red pepper *or* **1 jar (2 ounces)**
 sliced pimientos, drained
1 cup low-fat milk
3 eggs
3 tablespoons chopped fresh chives or green onion tops *or*
 ¾ teaspoon dried thyme or oregano leaves
 Salsa and low-fat sour cream or plain yogurt (optional)

Heat oven to 375°F. Grease 8- or 9-inch square baking dish or other small casserole. Peel potatoes and slice very thinly; arrange half of potatoes in baking dish. Sprinkle with salt and black pepper. Cover with half of sausage. Arrange remaining potatoes on top; sprinkle with salt and black pepper. Top with remaining sausage and roasted red pepper.

Beat milk, eggs and chives until blended. Pour over potatoes. Cover baking dish with foil and bake 35 to 45 minutes or until potatoes are tender. Uncover and bake 5 to 10 minutes more. Serve with salsa and sour cream, if desired. *Makes 4 to 5 servings*

Favorite recipe from Colorado Potato Administrative Committee

French Toast Strata

**4 ounces day-old French or Italian bread, cut into
   ¾-inch cubes (4 cups)**
⅓ cup golden raisins
1 package (3 ounces) cream cheese, cut into ¼-inch cubes
3 eggs
1½ cups milk
½ cup maple-flavored pancake syrup
1 teaspoon vanilla
2 tablespoons sugar
1 teaspoon ground cinnamon
Additional maple-flavored pancake syrup (optional)

1. Spray 11×7-inch baking dish with nonstick cooking spray. Place bread cubes in even layer in prepared dish; sprinkle raisins and cream cheese evenly over bread.

2. Beat eggs in medium bowl with electric mixer at medium speed until blended. Add milk, ½ cup pancake syrup and vanilla; mix well. Pour egg mixture evenly over bread mixture. Cover; refrigerate at least 4 hours or overnight.

3. Preheat oven to 350°F. Combine sugar and cinnamon in small bowl; sprinkle evenly over strata.

4. Bake, uncovered, 40 to 45 minutes or until puffed, golden brown and knife inserted into center comes out clean. Cut into squares and serve with additional pancake syrup. *Makes 6 servings*

Serving Suggestion: Serve with fresh fruit compote.

Overnight Ham and Cheese Strata

12 slices white bread, crust removed
1 (10-ounce) package frozen chopped broccoli, thawed and
    drained
2 (5-ounce) cans HORMEL® chunk ham, drained and flaked
6 eggs, beaten
2 cups milk
¼ cup minced onion
¼ teaspoon dry mustard
3 cups shredded Cheddar cheese

Cut bread into small cubes. Layer one-half of bread cubes, broccoli and chunk ham in buttered 13×9-inch baking dish. Top with remaining bread cubes. Beat together eggs, milk, onion and dry mustard. Pour over bread. Sprinkle with cheese. Cover and refrigerate overnight. Heat oven to 325°F. Bake 55 to 60 minutes or until eggs are set.

Makes 12 servings

Weekend Brunch Casserole

1 pound BOB EVANS® Original Recipe Roll Sausage
1 can (8 ounces) refrigerated crescent dinner rolls
2 cups (8 ounces) shredded mozzarella cheese
4 eggs, beaten
¾ cup milk
¼ teaspoon salt
⅛ teaspoon black pepper

Preheat oven to 425°F. Crumble sausage into medium skillet. Cook over medium heat until browned, stirring occasionally. Drain off any drippings. Line bottom of greased 13×9-inch baking dish with crescent roll dough, firmly pressing perforations to seal. Sprinkle with sausage and cheese. Combine remaining ingredients in medium bowl until blended; pour over sausage. Bake 15 minutes or until set. Let stand 5 minutes before cutting into squares; serve hot. Refrigerate leftovers.

Makes 6 to 8 servings

Serving Suggestion: Serve with fresh fruit or sliced tomatoes.

Mushroom & Onion Egg Bake

1 tablespoon vegetable oil
4 ounces sliced mushrooms
4 green onions, chopped
1 cup cottage cheese
6 eggs
1 cup sour cream
2 tablespoons all-purpose flour
¼ teaspoon salt
⅛ teaspoon black pepper
  Dash hot pepper sauce

1. Preheat oven to 350°F. Grease shallow 1-quart baking dish.

2. Heat oil in medium skillet over medium heat. Add mushrooms and onions; cook until tender. Set aside.

3. In blender or food processor, blend cottage cheese until almost smooth. Add eggs, sour cream, flour, salt, black pepper and hot pepper sauce; blend until combined. Stir in onions and mushrooms. Pour into prepared baking dish. Bake about 40 minutes or until knife inserted near center comes out clean.   *Makes about 6 servings*

Cottage cheese is a highly perishable
fresh cheese. Store it in the coldest part
of the refrigerator for up to 10 days past
the sell-by date stamped on the carton.

Baked Eggs Florentine

2 packages (10 ounces each) frozen creamed spinach
4 slices (⅛ inch thick) deli ham, about 5 to 6 ounces
4 eggs
   Salt and black pepper
⅛ teaspoon ground nutmeg
½ cup (2 ounces) shredded provolone cheese
2 tablespoons chopped roasted red pepper

1. Preheat oven to 450°F. Make small cut in each package of spinach. Microwave on HIGH 5 to 6 minutes, turning packages halfway through cooking time.

2. Meanwhile, grease 8-inch square baking pan. Place ham slices on bottom of prepared pan, overlapping slightly. Spread spinach over ham slices.

3. Make 4 indentations in spinach. Carefully break 1 egg in each. Season with salt and black pepper. Sprinkle with nutmeg.

4. Bake 16 to 19 minutes or until eggs are set. Remove from oven. Sprinkle cheese and red pepper over top. Return to oven and bake 1 to 2 minutes longer or until cheese is melted. Serve immediately.

Makes 4 servings

Serving Suggestion: Serve with toasted English muffin halves and fresh pineapple pieces.

Prep and Cook Time: 28 minutes

Ham and Cheese Baked Frittata

> 6 tablespoons CRISCO® Oil*
> 4 cups frozen shredded potatoes or 4 Idaho or russet
>   potatoes, peeled and shredded
> 1½ teaspoons salt, divided
> ½ teaspoon freshly ground black pepper
> 1 pound baked ham, cut into ½-inch cubes
> 12 eggs
> 6 tablespoons milk
> ½ teaspoon Italian seasoning
> 2 cups (8 ounces) shredded Cheddar, Monterey Jack or
>   Swiss cheese
> 1½ cups chunky salsa, heated

Use your favorite Crisco Oil.

Heat oven to 350°F.

Heat oil in 10- or 12-inch skillet on medium heat. Add potatoes; sprinkle with ½ teaspoon salt and pepper. Cook 8 minutes or until almost brown. Add ham and cook 2 to 3 minutes longer.

Meanwhile, beat eggs with milk, Italian seasoning and remaining 1 teaspoon salt. Place potato mixture in 13×9-inch casserole sprayed with CRISCO No-Stick Cooking Spray. Stir egg mixture into potatoes.

Bake covered for 15 minutes. Remove from oven. Remove cover, sprinkle with cheese and return to oven. Bake 15 minutes more or until cheese is melted and eggs are set. Turn oven to broil and continue to cook about 2 minutes or until top is browned. Allow to cool 10 minutes before cutting into 8 squares. Serve with heated salsa.
Makes 8 servings

Apple Brunch Strata

½ **pound sausage, casing removed**
4 **cups cubed French bread**
2 **cups diced peeled Michigan Apples**
¼ **cup sliced green onions**
⅓ **cup sliced black olives**
1½ **cups (6 ounces) shredded sharp Cheddar cheese**
2 **cups reduced-fat milk**
8 **eggs**
2 **teaspoons spicy brown mustard**
½ **teaspoon salt**
¼ **teaspoon black pepper**
   Paprika

1. Brown sausage in skillet over medium-high heat. Drain on paper towels; set aside.

2. Spray 13×9×2-inch baking dish with nonstick cooking spray. Layer half of bread cubes in bottom of dish. Crumble sausage over bread. Top with Michigan Apples, green onions, olives and cheese. Place remaining bread cubes on top.

3. Mix milk, eggs, mustard, salt and pepper in medium bowl; pour over bread. Cover with foil and refrigerate 4 hours or overnight.

4. Preheat oven to 350°F. Bake, covered, 45 minutes. Remove foil and bake 15 minutes or until center is set. Let stand 15 minutes before serving. Sprinkle with paprika, if desired.   *Makes 8 servings*

Tip: Suggested Michigan Apple varieties to use include Empire, Gala, Golden Delicious, Ida Red, Jonagold, Jonathan, McIntosh and Rome.

Variation: Substitute 1 can (20 ounces) sliced Michigan Apples, drained and chopped for fresh Michigan Apples.

Favorite recipe from Michigan Apple Committee

Aunt Marilyn's Cinnamon French Toast Casserole

1 large loaf French bread, cut into 1½-inch slices
3½ cups milk
9 eggs
1½ cups sugar, divided
1 tablespoon vanilla
½ teaspoon salt
6 to 8 medium baking apples, such as McIntosh or Cortland, peeled and sliced
1 teaspoon ground cinnamon
½ teaspoon nutmeg

1. Place bread slices into greased 13×9-inch glass baking dish or casserole.

2. Whisk milk, eggs, 1 cup sugar, vanilla and salt in large bowl 30 seconds or until well combined. Pour half of mixture over bread.

3. Layer apple slices over bread. Pour remaining half of egg mixture over apples.

4. Mix remaining ½ cup sugar, cinnamon and nutmeg in small bowl; sprinkle over top. Cover and refrigerate overnight.

5. Bake, uncovered, at 350°F 1 hour until casserole is heated through and eggs are set.

Makes 6 to 8 servings

Make-Ahead Brunch Bake

1 pound bulk pork sausage
6 eggs, beaten
2 cups light cream or half-and-half
½ teaspoon salt
1 teaspoon ground mustard
1 cup (4 ounces) shredded Cheddar cheese, divided
1⅓ cups *French's*® French Fried Onions, divided

Crumble sausage into large skillet. Cook over medium-high heat until browned; drain well. Stir in eggs, cream, salt, mustard, *½ cup* cheese and ⅔ *cup* French Fried Onions; mix well. Pour into greased 12×8-inch baking dish. Refrigerate, covered, 8 hours or overnight. Bake, uncovered, at 350°F for 45 minutes or until knife inserted in center comes out clean. Top with remaining cheese and ⅔ *cup* onions; bake, uncovered, 5 minutes or until onions are golden brown. Let stand 15 minutes before serving.

Makes 6 servings

Microwave Directions: Crumble sausage into 12×8-inch microwave-safe dish. Cook, covered, on HIGH 4 to 6 minutes or until sausage is cooked. Stir sausage halfway through cooking time. Drain well. Stir in ingredients and refrigerate as above. Cook, covered, 10 to 15 minutes or until center is firm. Stir egg mixture halfway through cooking time. Top with remaining cheese and onions; cook, uncovered, 1 minute or until cheese melts. Let stand 5 minutes before serving.

Hash Brown Frittata

1 (10-ounce) package **BOB EVANS®** Skinless Link Sausage
6 eggs
1 (12-ounce) package frozen hash brown potatoes, thawed
1 cup (4 ounces) shredded Cheddar cheese
⅓ cup whipping cream
¼ cup chopped green and/or red bell pepper
¼ teaspoon salt
Dash black pepper

Preheat oven to 350°F. Cut sausage into bite-size pieces. Cook in small skillet over medium heat until lightly browned, stirring occasionally. Drain off any drippings. Whisk eggs in medium bowl; stir in sausage and remaining ingredients. Pour into greased 2-quart casserole dish. Bake, uncovered, 30 minutes or until eggs are almost set. Let stand 5 minutes before cutting into squares; serve hot. Refrigerate leftovers.

Makes 6 servings

Ham & Cheese Grits Soufflé

3 cups water
¾ cup quick-cooking grits
½ teaspoon salt
½ cup (2 ounces) shredded mozzarella cheese
2 ounces ham, finely chopped
2 tablespoons minced chives
2 eggs, separated
Dash hot pepper sauce

1. Preheat oven to 375°F. Grease 1½-quart soufflé dish or deep casserole.

2. Bring water to a boil in medium saucepan. Stir in grits and salt. Cook, stirring frequently, about 5 minutes or until thickened. Stir in cheese, ham, chives, egg yolks and hot pepper sauce.

3. Beat egg whites in small clean bowl until stiff but not dry; fold into grits mixture. Pour into prepared dish. Bake about 30 minutes or until puffed and golden. Serve immediately.

Makes 4 to 6 servings

Spicy Chicken Tortilla Casserole

- 1 tablespoon vegetable oil
- 1 cup chopped green bell pepper
- 1 small onion, chopped
- 2 cloves garlic, finely chopped
- 1 pound (about 4) boneless, skinless chicken breast halves, cut into bite-size pieces
- 1 jar (16 ounces) ORTEGA® Salsa (any flavor)
- 1 can (2¼ ounces) sliced ripe olives
- 6 corn tortillas, cut into halves
- 2 cups (8 ounces) shredded Monterey Jack or cheddar cheese
  Sour cream (optional)

PREHEAT oven to 350°F.

HEAT oil in large skillet over medium-high heat. Add bell pepper, onion and garlic; cook for 2 to 3 minutes or until vegetables are tender.

ADD chicken; cook, stirring frequently, for 3 to 5 minutes or until chicken is no longer pink in center. Stir in salsa and olives; remove from heat.

PLACE 6 tortilla halves onto bottom of ungreased 8-inch square baking pan. Top with half of chicken mixture and 1 cup cheese; repeat.

BAKE for 15 to 20 minutes or until bubbly. Serve with sour cream. *Makes 8 servings*

Mustard Chicken & Vegetables

¼ cup *French's*® Honey Dijon Mustard or Classic Yellow®
    Mustard
¼ cup vegetable oil
 1 tablespoon red wine vinegar
½ teaspoon dried oregano, crumbled
¼ teaspoon pepper
¼ teaspoon salt
 2 pounds chicken pieces, fat trimmed
 2 cups (8 ounces) fusilli or rotini, cooked in unsalted water
    and drained
 1 can (10¾ ounces) condensed cream of chicken soup
 1 cup *each* zucchini and yellow squash, cut into 1-inch chunks
½ cup milk
1⅓ cups *French's*® French Fried Onions, divided
 1 medium tomato, cut into wedges

Preheat oven to 375°F. In large bowl, combine mustard, oil, vinegar
and seasonings; mix well. Toss chicken in mustard sauce until coated.
Reserve remaining mustard sauce. Arrange chicken in 13×9-inch
baking dish. Bake, uncovered, at 375°F for 30 minutes. Stir hot pasta,
soup, squash, milk and ⅔ *cup* French Fried Onions into remaining
mustard sauce. Spoon pasta mixture into baking dish, placing it
under and around chicken. Bake, uncovered, 15 to 20 minutes or
until chicken is done. Top pasta mixture with tomato wedges and
top chicken with remaining ⅔ *cup* onions; bake, uncovered, 3 minutes
or until onions are golden brown.   *Makes 4 to 6 servings*

Microwave Directions: Prepare mustard sauce as above; add chicken
and toss until coated. Reserve remaining mustard sauce. In 12×8-inch
microwave-safe dish, arrange chicken with meatiest parts toward
edges of dish. Cook, uncovered, on HIGH 10 minutes. Rearrange
chicken. Prepare pasta mixture and add to chicken as above. Cook,
uncovered, 15 to 17 minutes or until chicken and vegetables are done.
Stir vegetables and pasta and rotate dish halfway through cooking
time. Top with tomato wedges and remaining onions as above; cook,
uncovered, 1 minute. Let stand 5 minutes.

Thanksgiving Pie

2½ cups prepared stuffing
1½ cups JENNIE-O TURKEY STORE® Turkey, cooked, cubed
¼ cup chopped onion
1 cup shredded Swiss cheese
4 eggs
¾ cup milk
2 teaspoons prepared mustard
¼ teaspoon pepper

Heat oven to 350°F. Pat stuffing evenly into greased 9-inch pie plate to form crust, building up sides to rim. Sprinkle turkey, onion, and cheese evenly over crust. In small bowl, combine eggs, milk, mustard and pepper; mix well. Pour over turkey. Bake 35 to 40 minutes or until knife inserted near center comes out clean. Let stand 5 minutes before cutting. *Makes 6 servings*

Prep Time: 30 minutes • Cook Time: 45 minutes

Herbed Chicken and Potatoes

2 medium all-purpose potatoes, thinly sliced (about 1 pound)
8 lemon slices (optional)
4 bone-in chicken breast halves (about 2 pounds)*
1 envelope LIPTON® RECIPE SECRETS® Savory Herb with Garlic Soup Mix
⅓ cup water
1 tablespoon BERTOLLI® Olive Oil

Substitution: Use 1 (2½- to 3-pound) chicken, cut into serving pieces.

1. Preheat oven to 375°F. In 13×9-inch baking or roasting pan, combine potatoes and lemon; arrange chicken on top.

2. Pour soup mix blended with water and oil over chicken and potatoes.

3. Bake 50 minutes or until chicken is thoroughly cooked and potatoes are tender. *Makes 4 servings*

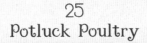

Chicken Hot Dish

 1 package (8 ounces) thin noodles or spaghetti
 3 tablespoons CRISCO® Oil*
 ½ cup chopped onion
 3 tablespoons PILLSBURY BEST® All-Purpose Flour
 1 tablespoon chopped fresh parsley
 ¼ teaspoon salt
 ¼ teaspoon pepper
 1½ cups chicken broth
 1 package (8 ounces) shredded Cheddar or Colby cheese,
    divided
 1 bag (16 ounces) frozen vegetables
 3 cups cubed cooked chicken

Use your favorite Crisco Oil.

1. Cook noodles according to package directions. Drain.

2. Heat oven to 350°F. Grease 3- to 4-quart baking dish.

3. Heat oil in medium saucepan on medium-high heat. Add onion. Cook until soft. Blend in flour, parsley, salt and pepper. Cook and stir for 1 minute. Add chicken broth. Cook and stir for 3 to 4 minutes or until mixture comes to a simmer. Reduce heat to low. Add 1½ cups cheese. Stir until just melted. Remove from heat.

4. Combine noodles, vegetables, chicken and cheese sauce in large bowl. Transfer to baking dish. Top with remaining ½ cup cheese.

5. Bake 30 minutes or until hot and bubbly. *Do not overbake.* Season with additional salt and pepper, if desired.   *Makes 12 servings*

Note: Casserole may be prepared a day ahead and refrigerated. Adjust baking time accordingly.

Turkey-Spaghetti Pie

6 ounces spaghetti, cooked according to package instructions and drained
⅓ cup grated Parmesan cheese
1 egg white, lightly beaten
2½ tablespoons margarine, melted, divided
1 cup chopped onion
1 clove garlic, minced
1 package (10 ounces) frozen mixed vegetables, thawed and drained
2 tablespoons flour
1 teaspoon poultry seasoning
⅛ teaspoon pepper
1½ cups skim milk
2 cups cubed cooked turkey

1. Preheat oven to 350°F.

2. In medium-size bowl combine spaghetti, cheese, egg white and 1 tablespoon margarine. In well-greased 9-inch pie plate, press spaghetti mixture over bottom and up side of pie plate. Grease 12×10-inch piece aluminum foil. Press foil, greased-side-down, on top of pasta shell. Bake 25 to 30 minutes or until pasta shell is set and slightly browned on edges.

3. In medium-size saucepan over medium-high heat, sauté onion and garlic in remaining margarine 2 to 3 minutes or until onion is translucent. Fold in vegetables and cook for 1 minute. Sprinkle flour, poultry seasoning and pepper over mixture, stirring to combine. Remove pan from heat.

4. Slowly pour milk over vegetable mixture, stirring constantly. Return saucepan to medium heat; cook and stir until mixture is thickened. Add turkey, reduce heat to medium-low and simmer 5 minutes or until heated throughout. Pour mixture into cooked pasta shell.

5. To serve, cut spaghetti pie into six wedges.   *Makes 6 servings*

Favorite recipe from National Turkey Federation

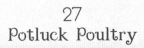

Spicy Chicken & Rice Bake

4 boneless, skinless chicken breast halves (about 1 pound)
1 jar (1 pound 10 ounces) RAGÚ® Robusto®! Pasta Sauce
2 cups water
⅔ cup uncooked white rice
½ cup sliced pitted ripe olives
1 tablespoon capers, drained and chopped
1 teaspoon salt
½ teaspoon ground black pepper
¼ teaspoon dried oregano leaves, crushed
⅛ teaspoon crushed red pepper flakes

Preheat oven to 375°F. In 13×9-inch casserole, combine all ingredients. Bake uncovered 40 minutes or until rice is tender and chicken is thoroughly cooked. *Makes 4 servings*

Classic Chicken Biscuit Pie

12 boneless, skinless chicken tenderloins, cut into 1-inch pieces
4 cups water
2 boxes UNCLE BEN'S® COUNTRY INN® Chicken
  Flavored Rice
1 bag (1 pound) frozen peas, potatoes and carrots
1 can (10¾ ounces) condensed cream of chicken soup
1 container (12 ounces) refrigerated buttermilk biscuits

1. Heat oven to 400°F. In large saucepan, combine chicken, water, rice, contents of seasoning packets, vegetable mixture and soup; mix well. Bring to a boil. Cover; reduce heat and simmer 10 minutes.

2. Place in 13×9-inch baking pan; top with biscuits.

3. Bake 10 to 12 minutes or until biscuits are golden brown.
Makes 8 to 10 servings

Tip: For individual pot pies, place rice mixture in small ramekins or casseroles. Proceed with recipe as directed.

Zesty Cheddar Casserole

2 packages (1½ ounces each) 4-cheese pasta sauce mix
2 cups milk
1 cup finely chopped celery
½ cup chopped onion
3 to 4 tablespoons *Frank's® RedHot®* Original Cayenne
    Pepper Sauce
1 bag (16 ounces) frozen vegetable combination such as
    broccoli, corn and red bell pepper
3 cups cooked diced chicken
6 slices crisply cooked bacon, crumbled
1½ cups (6 ounces) shredded Cheddar cheese, divided
1 package (7½ ounces) refrigerated buttermilk biscuits

1. Preheat oven to 375°F. Prepare sauce mix in 3-quart saucepan according to package directions using milk, 1 cup water and omitting butter. Add celery, onion and **Frank's RedHot** Sauce. Cook and stir 1 minute.

2. Stir in vegetable combination, chicken, bacon and 1 cup cheese. Spoon into greased 3-quart casserole; cover. Bake 30 minutes; stir. Cut biscuits in half crosswise; arrange around edge of casserole. Sprinkle remaining ½ cup cheese over biscuits.

3. Bake, uncovered, 15 minutes or until biscuits are golden brown.

Makes 8 servings

Prep Time: 25 minutes • Cook Time: 50 minutes

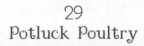

Italian BLT Chicken Strata

    8 slices bacon
    2 (16-ounce) packages PERDUE® Fit 'N Easy® Skinless
        & Boneless Chicken Breasts
   12 ounces focaccia bread, cut into ½-inch-thick slices
    2 large tomatoes, cored and sliced
    8 eggs or 2 cups egg substitute
  1½ cups heavy cream, light cream or milk
    1 teaspoon salt
      Pepper, to taste
    2 cups grated Cheddar cheese

Preheat oven to 350°F.

In a large skillet, cook bacon over medium heat. Drain on paper towels. Keeping a little bacon fat in pan, add chicken and cook until cooked through. Set aside.

Cover bottom of 13×9-inch baking dish with focaccia slices. Cover bread with tomato slices, then bacon. Cut chicken into thin slices and arrange over bacon. Top with remaining focaccia slices.

In large bowl, whisk together eggs, cream, salt and pepper. Pour mixture over strata and sprinkle top with cheese.

Bake 35 to 45 minutes or until cheese has melted and strata feels firm to the touch. Cut into 8 squares and serve hot.   *Makes 8 servings*

Prep Time: 25 minutes • Cook Time: 35 to 45 minutes

Quick Chopped Chicken and Artichoke Casserole

 4 boneless, skinless chicken breast halves
 1 can (13¾ ounces) water-packed artichoke hearts, drained
    and quartered
 1 can (8 ounces) sliced water chestnuts, drained
 1 cup mayonnaise
 ⅓ cup minced onion
 1 can (2 ounces) diced pimento
 ¼ teaspoon pepper
 ½ cup grated Parmesan cheese
 ⅓ cup dry seasoned bread crumbs

In medium saucepan, cover chicken with cold water. Bring to a boil. Reduce heat to low; simmer, covered, about 7 minutes. Turn off heat; remove cover and let chicken cool in water for 10 minutes.

While chicken is cooling, stir together artichoke hearts, water chestnuts, mayonnaise, onion, pimento and pepper in medium bowl. In small bowl, stir together Parmesan cheese and bread crumbs. Stir half the crumb mixture into artichoke mixture. Set remaining bread crumbs aside.

Preheat oven to 400°F. Dice chicken and stir into artichoke mixture. Spoon into 1½-quart casserole and smooth top. Sprinkle with reserved crumbs. Bake about 35 minutes or until golden brown and heated through. *Makes 4 servings*

Tip: To freeze, cover tightly with plastic wrap and freeze until needed. To thaw, transfer from freezer to refrigerator 12 to 24 hours in advance. Bake in preheated 400°F oven for about 40 minutes or until golden brown and heated through.

Favorite recipe from National Chicken Council

Triple Cheese & Turkey Tetrazzini

  1 (12-ounce) package extra broad egg noodles
  2 (10¾-ounce) cans cheddar cheese condensed soup
1½ cups skim milk
  4 teaspoons HERB-OX® chicken flavored bouillon, divided
  3 cups diced cooked turkey breast
  1 medium onion, chopped
1½ cups sourdough cheese-flavored croutons, crushed
  3 tablespoons butter, melted
1½ cups finely shredded Monterey Jack and Cheddar cheeses

Preheat oven to 350°F. Prepare noodles as package directs. Meanwhile, in saucepan, combine soup, milk and 3 teaspoons bouillon; heat over medium heat until warmed through. In large bowl, combine prepared egg noodles, turkey, onion and soup mixture. Stir to combine ingredients thoroughly. Place turkey mixture into a 13×9-inch baking dish lightly sprayed with nonstick cooking spray. In small bowl, toss crushed croutons with melted butter and remaining bouillon. Sprinkle cheese over noodles and top with crouton mixture. Bake 40 to 45 minutes or until warmed through and golden brown.   *Makes 12 servings*

Southwest Turkey Squares

  2 cups shredded Cheddar and Monterey Jack cheeses
  2 (5-ounce) cans HORMEL® chunk turkey, drained and flaked
  1 (4¼-ounce) can CHI-CHI'S® diced green chilies
⅓ cup minced fresh cilantro or 1½ teaspoons ground coriander
    Vegetable cooking spray
  6 eggs, beaten
    Sour cream (optional)
  1 tomato, chopped, seeded and drained (optional)

Heat oven to 350°F. Sprinkle cheese, turkey, green chilies and cilantro evenly in 11×7-inch baking dish coated with cooking spray. Pour eggs over mixture. Bake 25 to 30 minutes or until knife inserted into center comes out clean. Cool to room temperature. Cut into 1½-inch squares and garnish with sour cream and tomatoes, if desired.

Makes 24 appetizers

Broccoli Chicken Pasta Casserole

2 teaspoons CRISCO® Oil*
⅔ cup chopped onion
2 large cloves garlic, minced
1 pound boneless, skinless chicken breasts, cut into 1-inch pieces
2 cans (14½ ounces each) whole tomatoes, undrained and coarsely chopped
1 can (8 ounces) tomato sauce
¼ cup ketchup
1¼ teaspoons dried basil leaves
¾ teaspoon dried oregano leaves
¼ teaspoon salt
1 package (10 ounces) frozen broccoli cuts, thawed and well drained
5 ounces uncooked small macaroni, cooked (without salt or fat) and well drained
½ cup grated Parmesan cheese, divided

Use your favorite Crisco Oil.

1. Heat oven to 350°F. Place cooling rack on countertop.

2. Heat oil in large skillet on medium-high heat. Add onion and garlic. Cook and stir until tender. Add chicken. Cook and stir just until chicken is no longer pink in center. Stir in tomatoes, tomato sauce, ketchup, basil, oregano and salt. Bring to a boil. Reduce heat to low. Simmer 5 minutes, stirring occasionally.

4. Combine broccoli, macaroni, chicken mixture and ¼ cup cheese in large bowl. Stir well. Spoon into 13×9×2-inch baking dish. Sprinkle with remaining ¼ cup cheese.

5. Bake at 350°F for 20 minutes. *Do not overbake.* Remove dish to cooling rack. Serve warm.   *Makes 8 servings*

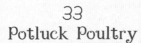

Shepherd's Pie

    1 tablespoon vegetable oil
    2 teaspoons bottled or fresh minced garlic
    1 package JENNIE-O TURKEY STORE® Lean Ground Turkey
    ½ teaspoon dried basil
    ½ teaspoon dried thyme
    ½ teaspoon salt
    ½ teaspoon freshly ground black pepper
    1 can (10½ ounces) *or* 1 jar (12 ounces) turkey gravy
    ½ cup frozen corn kernels
    ½ cup frozen tiny peas
 2½ cups prepared mashed potatoes, homemade or frozen
        prepared
    ½ cup (2 ounces) shredded Cheddar cheese

Heat oil in 10-inch ovenproof skillet over medium-high heat. (If skillet is not ovenproof, wrap handle in double thickness of aluminum foil.) Add garlic. Crumble turkey into skillet; sprinkle with herbs, salt and pepper. Cook 5 minutes or until no longer pink, stirring occasionally. Add gravy, corn and peas; simmer uncovered 5 minutes or until vegetables are defrosted and mixture is very hot. Spoon mashed potatoes around edge of mixture, leaving 3-inch opening in center. Sprinkle cheese over all. Transfer skillet to broiler and broil about 4 to 5 inches from heat source for 2 to 3 minutes or until cheese is melted and mixture is bubbly.   *Makes 6 servings*

For the best homemade mashed potatoes,
use Russets. One pound of potatoes (2 to
3 medium) will make 2 to 3 cups mashed.

One-Dish Chicken Florentine

4 boneless, skinless chicken breast halves (about 1¼ pounds)
1 jar (1 pound 10 ounces) RAGÚ® Old World Style® Pasta Sauce
1½ cups water
1¼ cups uncooked regular or converted rice
1 package (10 ounces) frozen chopped spinach, thawed
1 cup shredded mozzarella cheese (about 4 ounces)

1. Preheat oven to 375°F. Season chicken, if desired, with salt and pepper.

2. In 13×9-inch baking dish, combine Ragú Pasta Sauce, water, rice and spinach. Arrange chicken on uncooked rice mixture.

3. Bake uncovered 30 minutes. Sprinkle with cheese and bake an additional 10 minutes or until chicken is thoroughly cooked. Let stand 10 minutes before serving. *Makes 4 servings*

Prep Time: 5 minutes • Cook Time: 40 minutes

The Original Ranch® Tetrazzini

8 ounces linguine, cooked and drained
3 cups shredded cooked chicken
1½ cups prepared HIDDEN VALLEY® The Original Ranch® Dressing
½ cup dry white wine or chicken broth
1 jar (4½ ounces) sliced mushrooms, drained
¼ cup buttered* bread crumbs

Melt 1½ teaspoons butter; stir in plain dry bread crumbs until evenly coated.

Combine linguine, chicken, dressing, wine and mushrooms. Pour into 2-quart casserole dish. Top with crumbs. Bake at 350°F for 20 minutes or until bubbly around edges. *Makes 6 servings*

Tarragon Lemon Chicken

¼ cup all-purpose flour
  Salt and freshly ground black pepper
4 boneless skinless chicken breast halves
4 tablespoons FILIPPO BERIO® Olive Oil, divided
1 large onion, chopped
1 red bell pepper, seeded and cut into strips
2 ribs celery, thinly sliced
1 cup chicken broth
1 cup dry white wine
1 tablespoon chopped fresh tarragon *or* 1 teaspoon dried
  tarragon leaves
3 cloves garlic, crushed
  Finely grated peel and juice of 1 lemon
  Lemon slices and fresh tarragon sprigs (optional)

Preheat oven to 375°F. In small shallow bowl, combine flour with salt and black pepper to taste. Coat each chicken piece in flour mixture; reserve any remaining flour mixture. In large skillet, heat 2 tablespoons olive oil over medium heat until hot. Add onion, bell pepper and celery; cook and stir 5 minutes or until onion is soft. Remove onion mixture from skillet with slotted spoon; set aside.

Add remaining 2 tablespoons olive oil to skillet; heat over medium heat until hot. Add chicken; cook 5 minutes or until brown, turning occasionally. Add reserved flour mixture to skillet; mix well. Add chicken broth, wine, tarragon, garlic, lemon peel and lemon juice; bring to a boil. Return onion mixture to skillet; mix well. Transfer mixture to large casserole. Cover with foil. Bake 40 minutes or until chicken is no longer pink in center and juices run clear. Garnish with lemon slices and tarragon, if desired.   *Makes 4 servings*

Rotini and Turkey Mozzarella

   8 ounces dry rotini
   2 tablespoons olive or vegetable oil
1½ cups thinly sliced zucchini
   1 cup chopped onion
   2 cloves garlic, minced
   1 can (28 ounces) CONTADINA® Recipe Ready Crushed
      Tomatoes
   2 cups cubed, cooked turkey, chicken, ham or smoked turkey
   ¾ cup whole kernel corn
   2 teaspoons Italian herb seasoning
   ½ teaspoon salt
   ¼ teaspoon ground black pepper
1½ cups (6 ounces) shredded mozzarella cheese
   ⅔ cup (about 3 ounces) grated Parmesan cheese
   3 tablespoons chopped fresh parsley *or* 1 teaspoon dried
      parsley flakes

1. Cook pasta according to package directions; drain.

2. Meanwhile, heat oil in large skillet. Add zucchini, onion and garlic; sauté for 3 to 5 minutes or until vegetables are tender. Stir in crushed tomatoes, turkey, corn, Italian seasoning, salt and pepper.

3. Bring to a boil. Reduce heat to low; simmer, uncovered, for 5 minutes or until heated through.

4. Remove from heat; stir in pasta. Spoon half of pasta mixture into greased 13×9-inch baking dish; top with half of mozzarella and Parmesan cheeses. Repeat layers.

5. Bake in preheated 350°F oven for 20 to 25 minutes or until heated through. Let stand for 5 minutes. Sprinkle with parsley just before serving. *Makes 8 servings*

Prep Time: 8 minutes • Cook Time: 37 minutes

Snappy Pea and Chicken Pot Pie

  2½ cups chicken broth
  1 medium baking potato, peeled and cut into ½-inch chunks
1½ cups sliced carrots (½-inch slices)
  1 cup frozen pearl onions
  ½ teaspoon dried rosemary
  ½ teaspoon TABASCO® brand Pepper Sauce
  ¼ teaspoon salt
  1 medium red bell pepper, coarsely diced
  4 ounces (about 1 cup) sugar-snap peas, trimmed and halved
      lengthwise
  3 tablespoons butter or margarine
  ¼ cup flour
  8 ounces cooked chicken breast meat, cut in 3×1-inch strips
  1 sheet frozen puff pastry, thawed
  1 egg, beaten with 1 teaspoon water

In large saucepan bring chicken broth to a boil over high heat. Add potato, carrots, pearl onions, rosemary, TABASCO® Sauce and salt. Reduce heat to medium; cover and simmer 8 to 10 minutes until vegetables are tender. Add bell pepper and sugar-snap peas; boil 30 seconds, just until peas turn bright green. Drain vegetables, reserving chicken broth; set aside.

Melt butter in saucepan over low heat. Stir in flour and cook 3 to 4 minutes, stirring constantly. Pour in 2 cups of reserved chicken broth and whisk until smooth. Bring to a boil over medium heat, stirring constantly. Reduce heat to low and simmer 5 minutes, stirring frequently, until thickened and bubbly.

Arrange chicken strips in bottoms of four lightly buttered ramekins or soufflé dishes. Top chicken with vegetables and sauce.

Heat oven to 475°F. Unfold puff pastry on floured surface according to package directions. Cut pastry into four rectangles. Brush outside rims of ramekins with some of beaten egg mixture. Place pastry rectangle over each ramekin and press firmly around edges to seal. Trim dough and flute edges. Brush tops with remaining beaten egg mixture.

Place ramekins on baking sheet and bake 10 to 12 minutes or until pastry is puffed and well browned. Serve at once.   *Makes 4 servings*

Sunday Dinner Casserole

2 cups sweet onions, sliced into rings
½ cup cooking sherry
2 tablespoons sugar
2 tablespoons balsamic vinegar
1 teaspoon dried thyme
½ teaspoon black pepper
2 cups egg noodles, cooked and drained
2 pounds boneless skinless chicken breasts
3 cups chicken broth
1 can (14½ ounces) diced tomatoes, drained
2 cloves garlic, minced
½ teaspoon red pepper flakes
¼ cup chopped fresh basil
2 teaspoons grated lemon peel

1. Preheat oven to 400°F.

2. Combine onions, sherry, sugar, vinegar, thyme and black pepper in large skillet. Cook over medium heat, stirring occasionally, until onions begin to brown.

3. Meanwhile, place noodles in 13×9-inch baking dish. Top with chicken breasts.

4. Combine broth, tomatoes, garlic and red pepper flakes with onions in skillet. Pour over chicken.

5. Bake, uncovered, 20 minutes; turn chicken breasts. Bake 20 to 25 minutes more or until chicken is no longer pink in center and juices run clear. Sprinkle with basil and lemon peel.

Makes 4 to 6 servings

Green Bean & Turkey Bake

1 can (10¾ ounces) condensed cream of mushroom soup
¾ cup milk
⅛ teaspoon pepper
2 packages (9 ounces each) frozen cut green beans, thawed
2 cups (12 ounces) cubed cooked turkey or chicken
1⅓ cups *French's*® French Fried Onions, divided
1½ cups (6 ounces) shredded Cheddar cheese, divided
3 cups hot mashed potatoes

1. Preheat oven to 375°F. In 3-quart casserole, combine soup, milk and pepper; mix well. Stir in beans, turkey, *⅔ cup* French Fried Onions and *1 cup* cheese. Spoon mashed potatoes on top.

2. Bake, uncovered, 45 minutes or until hot. Sprinkle with remaining *½ cup* cheese and *⅔ cup* onions. Bake 3 minutes or until onions are golden.   *Makes 6 servings*

Microwave Directions: Prepare mixture as above except do not top with potatoes. Cover casserole with vented plastic wrap. Microwave on HIGH 15 minutes or until heated through, stirring halfway through cooking time. Uncover. Top with mashed potatoes, remaining cheese and onions. Microwave on HIGH 2 to 4 minutes. Let stand 5 minutes.

Tip: Two (14½-ounce) cans cut green beans (drained) can be used instead of frozen beans. You can substitute instant mashed potatoes prepared according to package directions for 6 servings.

Prep Time: 10 minutes • Cook Time: 50 minutes

Tortilla Chicken Bake

**1 can (14½ ounces) DEL MONTE® Stewed Tomatoes -
Seasoned with Garlic, Jalapenos, & Mexican Spices**
½ cup chopped onion
2 cloves garlic, crushed
½ teaspoon dried oregano, crushed
½ teaspoon chili powder
½ pound boneless chicken, skinned and cut into strips
4 cups tortilla chips
**¾ cup shredded Monterey Jack cheese with jalapeño peppers
or Cheddar cheese**

1. Preheat oven to 375°F. Drain tomatoes, reserving liquid; chop tomatoes.

2. Combine reserved liquid, onion, garlic, oregano and chili powder in large skillet; boil 5 minutes, stirring occasionally.

3. Stir in tomatoes and chicken; cook over medium heat until chicken is no longer pink, about 5 minutes. Layer half of chips, chicken mixture and cheese in shallow 2-quart baking dish; repeat layers ending with cheese.

4. Cover and bake 15 minutes or until heated through. Serve with sour cream, if desired. *Makes 4 servings*

Prep Time: 3 minutes • Cook Time: 25 minutes

If you don't know the size of your baking
dish, it's easy to figure out. Simply fill the
empty dish with water and then measure
the amount of liquid needed to fill it.

Apple Curry Chicken

    4 boneless skinless chicken breasts
    1 cup apple juice, divided
    ¼ teaspoon salt
    Dash black pepper
1½ cups plain croutons
    1 medium apple, chopped
    1 medium onion, chopped
    ¼ cup raisins
    2 teaspoons brown sugar
    1 teaspoon curry powder
    ¾ teaspoon poultry seasoning
    ⅛ teaspoon garlic powder
    Apple slices and fresh thyme (optional)

1. Preheat oven to 350°F. Lightly grease 2-quart round baking dish.

2. Arrange chicken breasts in single layer in prepared dish.

3. Combine ¼ cup apple juice, salt and pepper in small bowl. Brush juice mixture over chicken.

4. Combine croutons, apple, onion, raisins, brown sugar, curry powder, poultry seasoning and garlic powder in large bowl. Toss with remaining ¾ cup apple juice.

5. Spread crouton mixture over chicken. Cover with foil; bake 45 minutes or until chicken is tender and no longer pink in center. Garnish with apple and thyme. *Makes 4 servings*

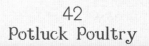

Easy Tex~Mex Bake

8 ounces uncooked thin mostaccioli
Nonstick cooking spray
1 pound ground turkey breast
⅔ cup prepared medium or mild salsa
1 package (10 ounces) frozen corn, thawed and drained
1 container (16 ounces) cottage cheese
1 egg
1 tablespoon minced fresh cilantro
½ teaspoon white pepper
¼ teaspoon ground cumin
½ cup (2 ounces) shredded Monterey Jack cheese

1. Cook pasta according to package directions. Drain and rinse well; set aside.

2. Spray large nonstick skillet with cooking spray. Add turkey; cook about 5 minutes or until no longer pink. Stir in salsa and corn. Remove from heat.

3. Preheat oven to 350°F. Combine cottage cheese, egg, cilantro, white pepper and cumin in small bowl.

4. Spoon half of turkey mixture on bottom of 11×7-inch or 2-quart baking dish. Top with pasta. Spoon cottage cheese mixture over pasta. Top with remaining turkey mixture. Sprinkle with Monterey Jack cheese.

5. Bake 25 to 30 minutes or until heated through. *Makes 6 servings*

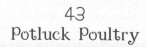

Wild Rice Country Casserole

1 cup chopped onion
¼ cup butter or margarine
1¼ pounds ground turkey
¼ teaspoon black pepper
4 cups frozen potatoes O'Brien with onions and peppers, thawed
3 cups cooked wild rice
2 cups shredded mild Cheddar cheese, divided
1 can (10¾ ounces) condensed cream of chicken soup
1 cup sour cream
⅓ cup bread crumbs

Preheat oven to 350°F. In large skillet, sauté onion in butter; remove from skillet. In same skillet, brown turkey. Sprinkle with pepper. Spread potatoes in greased 13×9-inch baking pan. Combine onion, turkey, wild rice, 1½ cups cheese, soup and sour cream in large bowl. Spread turkey mixture over potatoes. Sprinkle remaining ½ cup cheese and bread crumbs on top. Bake 40 minutes.   *Makes 8 servings*

Favorite recipe from Minnesota Cultivated Wild Rice Council

Cheesy Turkey Veg•All® Bake

1 package (5½ ounces) au gratin potato mix
2⅔ cups boiling water
1 can (15 ounces) VEG•ALL® Original Mixed Vegetables, drained
1 cup cubed cooked turkey
2 tablespoons butter

Preheat oven to 350°F. Place au gratin potato mix and sauce packet into large mixing bowl. Add water, Veg•All, turkey and butter; mix well. Pour into ungreased 2-quart casserole. Bake for 20 minutes or until top is golden brown. Cool for 5 minutes before serving.

Makes 6 servings

Prep Time: 7 minutes • Cook Time: 20 minutes

Chicken Lasagne Rolls

8 uncooked lasagne noodles
1 package (10 ounces) frozen chopped spinach, thawed
2 cups chopped cooked chicken
1½ cups lowfat cottage cheese
3 sliced green onions
2 tablespoons diced pimiento
½ teaspoon salt
¼ teaspoon black pepper
1 jar (12 ounces) HEINZ® HomeStyle or Fat Free Classic
   Chicken Gravy
1 can (4 ounces) sliced mushrooms, drained
1 cup finely shredded Swiss or mozzarella cheese, divided
   Paprika

Cook lasagne noodles according to package directions; set aside.
Squeeze spinach dry. In small bowl, combine spinach, chicken, cottage
cheese, onions, pimiento, salt and pepper. Spread about ½ cup spinach
mixture on each noodle; roll up jelly-roll fashion. Place seam-side
down in lightly greased 13×9-inch baking pan. Combine gravy,
mushrooms and ½ cup Swiss cheese; pour over rolls. Cover; bake in
preheated 350°F oven 40 to 45 minutes. Sprinkle with remaining
½ cup Swiss cheese and paprika. Bake an additional 10 to 15 minutes
or until cheese is melted and rolls are heated through.

Makes 4 to 6 servings

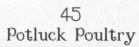

Spicy Turkey Casserole

1 tablespoon olive oil
1 pound turkey breast cutlets, cut into ½-inch pieces
2 spicy chicken or turkey sausages (about 3 ounces each),
    sliced ½ inch thick
1 cup diced green bell pepper
½ cup sliced mushrooms
½ cup diced onion
1 jalapeño pepper,* seeded and minced (optional)
½ cup chicken broth or water
1 can (14½ ounces) diced tomatoes, undrained
1 teaspoon Italian seasoning
¼ teaspoon black pepper
½ teaspoon paprika
1 cup cooked egg noodles
6 tablespoons grated Parmesan cheese
2 tablespoons coarse bread crumbs

*Jalapeño peppers can sting and irritate the skin; wear rubber gloves when handling peppers and do not touch eyes. Wash hands after handling peppers.

1. Preheat oven to 350°F. Heat oil in large nonstick skillet. Add turkey and sausages; cook and stir over medium heat 2 minutes. Add bell pepper, mushrooms, onion and jalapeño pepper. Cook and stir 5 minutes. Add chicken broth; cook 1 minute, scraping any browned bits from bottom of skillet. Add tomatoes with juice, seasonings and noodles.

2. Spoon turkey mixture into shallow 10-inch round casserole. Sprinkle with cheese and bread crumbs. Bake 15 to 20 minutes or until mixture is hot and bread crumbs are brown. Garnish as desired.
Makes 6 (1-cup) servings

Deep Dish Chicken Pot Pie

1 (15-ounce) package refrigerated pie crusts
½ cup chopped onion
¼ cup (½ stick) butter or margarine
⅓ cup all-purpose flour
1 tablespoon HERB-OX® chicken flavored bouillon, divided
¼ teaspoon dried thyme leaves
⅛ teaspoon ground black pepper
2 cups water
¾ cup milk
2½ cups diced cooked chicken
1 (10-ounce) package frozen mixed vegetables, thawed and drained
1 (2-ounce) jar diced pimento
2 tablespoons chopped fresh parsley

Heat oven to 400°F. Place one crust into 10-inch deep pie plate. In large saucepan, cook onion in butter until tender. Stir in flour, bouillon, thyme and pepper. Add water and milk all at once. Cook and stir until thickened and bubbly. Stir in chicken, mixed vegetables, pimento and parsley. Pour mixture into prepared crust. Place top crust over chicken mixture. Flute edges of pastry and cut slits in top to allow steam to escape. Bake 25 to 30 minutes or until crust is golden brown and filling is hot.   *Makes 6 to 8 servings*

Prep Time: 20 minutes • Total Time: 50 minutes

Lawry's® California Center Chicken Enchiladas

2 tablespoons vegetable oil
1 medium onion, chopped
3 to 4 cups cooked shredded chicken or turkey
1 can (14½ ounces) diced tomatoes, in juice
1 can (8 ounces) tomato sauce
1 can (4 ounces) diced green chiles
1 package (1.0 ounce) LAWRY'S® Taco Spices & Seasonings
½ teaspoon LAWRY'S® Seasoned Salt
¼ teaspoon LAWRY'S® Garlic Powder With Parsley
12 corn tortillas
2 cans (2¼ ounces each) sliced black olives, drained
5 cups shredded Monterey Jack cheese

In large skillet, heat oil. Add onion and cook over medium-high heat until tender. Add chicken, tomatoes, tomato sauce, chiles, Taco Spices & Seasonings, Seasoned Salt and Garlic Powder With Parsley; mix well. Bring to a boil; reduce heat to low, cover and cook for 15 to 20 minutes. In greased 13×9×2-inch baking dish, place 4 corn tortillas. Pour ⅓ of chicken mixture over tortillas, spreading evenly. Layer with ⅓ of olives and ⅓ of cheese. Repeat layers 2 times ending with cheese. Bake, uncovered, in 350°F oven for 30 to 40 minutes.

Makes 6 servings

Meal Idea: Serve with Mexican rice and a tossed green salad.

Prep Time: 15 minutes • Cook Time: 1 hour

Swiss Chicken Gratin

1 (10¾ ounce) can condensed cream of mushroom, chicken or celery soup, undiluted
¼ cup white wine, dry Vermouth or milk
1 (9-to 10-ounce) package fresh or frozen cooked chicken, thawed, cut into strips or chunks *or* 2 cups leftover rotisserie chicken, cut into chunks
¼ cup sliced green onions
2 BAYS® English Muffins, cut into 1-inch chunks
1 cup shredded Swiss cheese
⅛ teaspoon nutmeg
Paprika (optional)

Preheat oven to 375° F. Combine soup and wine in large bowl; mix well. Add chicken and green onions; mix well. Spread mixture into 1½-quart (11×7-inch) baking dish. Top with muffins and cheese. Sprinkle nutmeg and paprika, if desired, over top of casserole. Bake for 20 to 25 minutes or until golden brown and bubbly.

Makes 4 servings

Prep Time: 10 minutes • Bake Time: 25 minutes

Turkey Broccoli Bake

1 bag (16 ounces) frozen broccoli cuts, thawed, drained
2 cups cubed cooked turkey or chicken
2 cups soft bread cubes
8 ounces sliced American cheese
1 jar (12 ounces) HEINZ® HomeStyle Turkey or Chicken Gravy
½ cup undiluted evaporated milk
Dash pepper

In buttered 9-inch square baking dish, layer broccoli, turkey, bread cubes and cheese. Combine gravy, milk and pepper; pour over cheese. Bake in 375°F oven 40 minutes. Let stand 5 minutes.

Makes 6 servings

Creamy Creole Turkey Bake

⅔ cup chopped onion
⅔ cup chopped celery
⅓ cup chopped green pepper
 1 garlic clove, minced
 1 tablespoon margarine
¼ pound button mushrooms, sliced and cleaned
 4 ounces light cream cheese, softened
 1 can (8 ounces) low-sodium stewed tomatoes, drained
1½ teaspoons creole seasoning
 4 ounces uncooked fettucini, cooked according to package
    directions
 2 cups ½-inch cubed cooked turkey
    Vegetable cooking spray
¼ cup grated Parmesan cheese

1. In medium nonstick skillet over medium-high heat, sauté onion, celery, green pepper and garlic in margarine 4 to 5 minutes or until vegetables are crisp-tender. Add mushrooms and sauté 2 minutes. Remove from heat.

2. In medium bowl blend cream cheese, tomatoes and creole seasoning. Fold in vegetable mixture, fettucini and turkey.

3. Pour mixture into 9-inch square dish sprayed with vegetable cooking spray. Sprinkle cheese over top and bake in preheated 325°F oven for 30 minutes or until bubbly.   *Makes 4 servings*

Favorite recipe from National Turkey Federation

Turkey Enchilada Pie

¾ pound ground turkey
2 teaspoons vegetable oil
1 can (14½ ounces) DEL MONTE® Diced Tomatoes with
  Zesty Mild Green Chilies
1 package (1¼ ounces) taco seasoning mix
½ cup sliced green onions
1 can (2¼ ounces) sliced ripe olives, drained
6 corn tortillas
1½ cups shredded sharp Cheddar cheese

1. Brown meat in oil in large skillet over medium-high heat. Stir in tomatoes and taco seasoning mix.

2. Reduce heat; cover and cook 10 minutes, stirring occasionally. Stir in green onions and olives.

3. Place 1 tortilla in bottom of 2-quart baking dish; cover with about ½ cup meat sauce. Top with about ¼ cup cheese. Repeat, making six-layer stack.

4. Pour ½ cup water down edge, into bottom of dish. Cover with foil and bake at 425°F 30 minutes or until heated through. Cut into 4 wedges. Garnish with sour cream, if desired.   *Makes 4 servings*

Prep Time: 15 minutes • Cook Time: 48 minutes

Quick & Easy Lasagna

1 package JENNIE-O TURKEY STORE® Hot or Sweet Lean Italian Sausage

1 jar (26 ounces) tomato and basil or mushroom spaghetti sauce

6 (7×4-inch) no-boil lasagna noodles

1 container (15 ounces) ricotta cheese

¼ cup grated Parmesan cheese

2 cups (8 ounces) shredded mozzarella cheese

Heat oven to 450°F. Crumble sausage into large saucepan; discard casings. Cook over medium-high heat 5 minutes, breaking sausage into chunks and stirring frequently. Add spaghetti sauce; bring to a boil. Reduce heat; simmer uncovered 5 minutes, stirring occasionally. Spread ¾ cup sauce in bottom of 9-inch square baking dish. Arrange 2 noodles side by side over sauce. Combine ricotta cheese and Parmesan cheese; spoon half of mixture over noodles and top with 1 cup sauce and ½ cup mozzarella cheese. Repeat layering with 2 more noodles, pressing firmly, remaining ricotta cheese mixture, 1 cup sauce, ½ cup mozzarella cheese and last 2 noodles, pressing firmly. Top with remaining sauce. Cover with foil; bake for 25 minutes or until noodles are tender and sauce is bubbly. Uncover; top with remaining 1 cup mozzarella cheese. Return to oven; bake 5 minutes or until cheese is melted. Let stand 5 minutes before serving.

Makes 6 servings

Prep Time: 30 minutes • Cook Time: 30 minutes

Lattice-Top Chicken

1 can (10¾ ounces) condensed cream of potato soup
1¼ cups milk
½ teaspoon seasoned salt
1½ cups (7 ounces) cubed cooked chicken
1 bag (16 ounces) frozen vegetable combination (broccoli, carrots, cauliflower), thawed and drained
1 cup (4 ounces) shredded Cheddar cheese, divided
1⅓ cups *French's*® French Fried Onions, divided
1 cup biscuit baking mix*
¼ cup milk
1 egg, slightly beaten

*One package (4 ounces) refrigerated crescent rolls can be substituted for baking mix, ¼ cup milk and egg. Separate dough into 2 rectangles; press together perforated cuts. Cut each rectangle lengthwise into 3 strips. Arrange strips on hot chicken mixture to form lattice. Top as directed. Bake, uncovered, at 375°F for 15 to 20 minutes or until lattice is golden brown.

Preheat oven to 375°F. In large bowl, combine soup, 1¼ cups milk, seasoned salt, chicken, vegetables, ½ cup cheese and ⅔ *cup* French Fried Onions. Pour into 12×8-inch baking dish. Bake, covered, at 375°F for 15 minutes. Meanwhile, in small bowl, combine baking mix, ¼ cup milk and egg to form soft dough. Stir casserole and spoon dough over hot chicken mixture to form lattice design. Bake, uncovered, 20 to 25 minutes or until lattice is golden brown. Top lattice with remaining ½ cup cheese and ⅔ *cup* onions; bake, uncovered, 3 minutes or until onions are golden brown.   *Makes 4 to 6 servings*

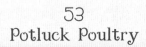

Scalloped Chicken & Pasta

¼ **cup margarine or butter, divided**
1 **package (6.2 ounces) PASTA RONI® Shells & White Cheddar**
2 **cups frozen mixed vegetables**
⅔ **cup milk**
2 **cups chopped cooked chicken or ham**
¼ **cup dry bread crumbs**

1. Preheat oven to 450°F.

2. In 3-quart saucepan, combine 2¼ cups water and 2 tablespoons margarine. Bring just to a boil. Stir in pasta and frozen vegetables. Reduce heat to medium.

3. Boil, uncovered, stirring frequently, 12 to 14 minutes or until most of water is absorbed. Add Special Seasonings, milk and chicken. Continue cooking 3 minutes.

4. Meanwhile, melt remaining 2 tablespoons margarine in small saucepan; stir in bread crumbs.

5. Transfer pasta mixture to 8- or 9-inch glass baking dish. Sprinkle with bread crumbs. Bake 10 minutes or until bread crumbs are browned and edges are bubbly.   *Makes 4 servings*

Chicken Rice Casserole

2 **cups 2% milk**
2 **tablespoons MRS. DASH® Minced Onion Medley**
¼ **cup butter**
2 **tablespoons all-purpose flour**
1 **can (7 ounces) sliced mushrooms, drained *or* 1 cup sliced fresh mushrooms**
¼ **cup chopped fresh parsley**
3 **cups cooked rice**
2 **cups cubed cooked chicken or turkey**
½ **cup diced cooked ham**
2 **cups coarsely chopped cooked broccoli**

Preheat oven to 350°F. Combine milk and Mrs. Dash® Minced Onion Medley in small saucepan or 2-cup glass microwavable measuring cup. Heat just until warm. Melt butter in large nonstick skillet over medium heat. Whisk in flour. Gradually whisk in milk mixture and heat until thickened; whisk constantly. Remove from heat and stir in mushrooms and parsley. Spray square glass 2-quart baking dish with nonstick coating spray. Layer rice, chicken, ham and broccoli in prepared dish. Pour sauce evenly over layered ingredients. Bake at 350°F for 25 to 30 minutes or until heated thoroughly.   *Makes 8 servings*

Prep Time: 10 minutes • Cook Time: 30 minutes

Pennsylvania Dutch Chicken Bake

 1 package (about 1¾ pounds) PERDUE® Fresh Skinless
    Chicken Thighs
    Salt and pepper to taste
 1 to 2 tablespoons canola oil
 1 can (14 to 16 ounces) sauerkraut, undrained
 1 can (14 to 15 ounces) whole onions, drained
 1 tart red apple, unpeeled and sliced
 6 to 8 dried whole apricots
 ½ cup raisins
 ¼ cup brown sugar, or to taste

Preheat oven to 350°F. Season thighs with salt and pepper. In large nonstick skillet over medium-high heat, heat oil. Cook thighs 6 to 8 minutes per side until browned. Meanwhile, in 12×9-inch shallow baking dish, mix sauerkraut, onions, apple, apricots, raisins and brown sugar until blended. Arrange thighs in sauerkraut mixture. Cover and bake 30 to 40 minutes or until chicken is cooked through and meat thermometer inserted in thickest part of thigh registers 180°F.
Makes 6 servings

Variation: If desired, substitute other fresh or dried fruit in this recipe, such as pears or pitted prunes.

Chicken Breasts Diavolo

6 chicken breast halves, boned, skinned and slightly flattened
½ cup finely minced fresh parsley
1 teaspoon lemon pepper seasoning
Dash salt
Dash garlic powder
3 tablespoons olive oil
3 (6-ounce) jars marinated artichoke hearts
1 tablespoon fresh lemon juice
1 (26-ounce) jar NEWMAN'S OWN® Diavolo Sauce
½ cup red wine (preferably Chianti)
1½ cups shredded mozzarella cheese
1½ cups onion-garlic flavor croutons (tossed with
     1 tablespoon olive oil)
6 cups hot cooked pasta or rice

Preheat oven to 350°F. Sprinkle chicken breasts with parsley, lemon pepper seasoning, salt and garlic powder. Roll up each breast, seasoned side in; secure with wooden toothpicks. Cook chicken in olive oil in large skillet until golden brown on all sides. Remove from pan with tongs and place in 13×9-inch baking dish. Carefully remove toothpicks.

Drain artichoke hearts; sprinkle with lemon juice and distribute among rolled chicken breasts.

Combine Newman's Own® Diavolo Sauce with wine; pour over chicken and artichokes. Sprinkle cheese evenly over top. Sprinkle with crouton mixture. Bake 30 to 40 minutes or until golden brown and bubbly.

Spoon chicken over pasta or rice. Serve with crusty Italian bread or rolls, a green salad and remaining red wine.   *Makes 6 servings*

Sweet Potato Turkey Pie

1 can (24 ounces) sweet potatoes, drained
2 tablespoons margarine, melted
¼ teaspoon pumpkin pie spice
   Nonstick vegetable cooking spray
2 cups cubed cooked turkey (½- to ¾-inch cubes)
1 can (10¾ ounces) reduced-fat, reduced-sodium cream of
   mushroom soup
1 package (9 ounces) frozen French-style green beans,
   thawed and drained
1 can (2 ounces) mushroom stems and pieces, drained
½ teaspoon *each* salt and pepper
2 tablespoons crushed canned French fried onion rings
1 can (8 ounces) cranberry sauce (optional)

1. In medium bowl blend sweet potatoes, margarine and pumpkin pie spice until smooth. Spray 9-inch pie plate with cooking spray. Line pie plate with potato mixture to form "pie shell;" set aside.

2. In medium bowl combine turkey, soup, beans, mushrooms, salt and pepper. Pour mixture into prepared shell. Sprinkle onions over top. Bake in preheated 350°F oven 30 minutes or until hot. Serve with cranberry sauce, if desired. *Makes 6 servings*

Favorite recipe from National Turkey Federation

Pumpkin pie spice is usually a blend
of ground cinnamon, ginger,
nutmeg and allspice.

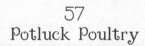

Meaty Meals

Baked Rigatoni

1 pound dry rigatoni
4 ounces mild Italian sausage, casings removed, sliced
1 cup chopped onion
2 cloves garlic, minced
1 can (14.5 ounces) CONTADINA® Recipe Ready
 Diced Tomatoes, undrained
1 can (6 ounces) CONTADINA Tomato Paste
1 cup chicken broth
1 teaspoon salt
1 cup (4 ounces) shredded mozzarella cheese, divided
½ cup (2 ounces) shredded Parmesan cheese (optional)
2 tablespoons chopped fresh basil or 2 teaspoons dried
 basil leaves, crushed

1. Cook pasta according to package directions. Drain and keep warm.

2. Meanwhile, cook sausage in large skillet for 4 to 6 minutes or until no longer pink. Remove sausage from skillet, reserving any drippings in skillet.

3. Add onion and garlic to skillet; sauté for 2 minutes. Stir in undrained tomatoes, tomato paste, broth and salt. Bring to a boil. Reduce heat to low; simmer, uncovered, for 10 minutes, stirring occasionally.

4. Combine pasta, tomato mixture, sausage, ½ cup mozzarella cheese, Parmesan cheese and basil in large bowl; spoon into ungreased 13×9-inch baking dish. Sprinkle with remaining mozzarella cheese. Bake in preheated 375°F oven for 10 to 15 minutes or until cheese is melted. *Makes 8 servings*

Baked Steak Flamenco

    ¼ **cup all-purpose flour**
    ½ **teaspoon seasoned salt**
    ⅛ **teaspoon ground black pepper**
 1½ **pounds trimmed round steak, cut into strips**
    ½ **cup thinly sliced onion**
   1 **cup thin green bell pepper rings**
   1 **cup sliced fresh mushrooms**
   1 **can (14.5 ounces) CONTADINA® Italian Style Stewed**
      Tomatoes, undrained
   ¼ **cup horseradish sauce**
   1 **tablespoon Worcestershire sauce**

1. Combine flour, seasoned salt and pepper in large plastic food storage bag, Add steak; shake to evenly coat.

2. Place in greased 13×9-inch baking dish. Arrange onion slices, bell pepper rings and mushrooms on top of meat.

3. Drain tomatoes, reserving juice. Slice tomatoes lengthwise; arrange on top of vegetables.

4. Combine reserved juice, horseradish sauce and Worcestershire sauce in small bowl; pour evenly over all ingredients in baking dish. Bake, uncovered, in preheated 350°F oven for 45 minutes to 1 hour or until desired doneness. Serve with hot cooked rice or potatoes, if desired.

Makes 6 servings

Ham with Spring Vegetables

1 can (10¾ ounces) condensed cream of celery soup, undiluted
¾ cup uncooked rice
1 tablespoon butter or margarine
1 to 1½ pounds HILLSHIRE FARM® Ham, cut into bite-size
**   pieces**
1 package (10 ounces) frozen mixed vegetables
1 can (4 ounces) sliced mushrooms, drained
1 cup (4 ounces) shredded Swiss cheese

Preheat oven to 350°F.

Combine soup, rice, ¾ cup water and butter in large skillet over medium
heat. Bring to a boil; reduce heat and simmer 5 minutes. Combine rice
mixture with Ham, vegetables and mushrooms in medium casserole;
sprinkle top with cheese. Bake, covered, 20 to 25 minutes or until rice is
cooked.   *Makes 4 servings*

Mexican Stuffed Shells

1 pound ground beef
1 jar (12 ounces) mild or medium picante sauce
1 can (8 ounces) tomato sauce
½ cup water
1 can (4 ounces) chopped green chilies, drained
1 cup (4 ounces) shredded Monterey Jack cheese, divided
1⅓ cups *French's*® French Fried Onions
12 pasta stuffing shells, cooked in unsalted water and drained

Preheat oven to 350°F. In large skillet, brown ground beef; drain. In
small bowl, combine picante sauce, tomato sauce and water. Stir
½ cup sauce mixture into beef along with chilies, ½ cup cheese and
⅔ *cup* French Fried Onions; mix well. Spread half of remaining sauce
mixture in bottom of 10-inch round baking dish. Stuff cooked shells
with beef mixture. Arrange shells in baking dish; top with remaining
sauce. Bake, covered, at 350°F for 30 minutes or until heated through.
Top with remaining ⅔ *cup* onions and cheese; bake, uncovered,
5 minutes or until cheese is melted.   *Makes 6 servings*

Baked Pasta with Beef and Beans

CRISCO® No-Stick Cooking Spray
3 tablespoons CRISCO® Oil*
1 small onion, peeled and chopped
2 teaspoons jarred minced garlic *or* 1 large garlic clove,
peeled and minced
1 pound ground beef *or* ½ pound ground beef and ½ pound
bulk Italian sausage
1 can (14½ ounces) chopped tomatoes, drained
2 tablespoons tomato paste
2 teaspoons Italian seasoning
½ teaspoon salt
¼ teaspoon freshly ground black pepper
½ pound penne pasta, cooked al dente
1 can (8 ounces) kidney beans, drained and rinsed
1 cup (4 ounces) shredded mozzarella or provolone cheese
¼ cup freshly grated Parmesan cheese

*Use your favorite Crisco Oil.

1. Heat oven to 400°F.

2. Spray 13×9 baking dish with CRISCO No Stick Cooking Spray. Set aside. Heat large skillet on medium-high heat. Add oil, onion, garlic and beef. Cook 3 minutes, breaking up with fork, or until onion is soft and beef is no longer pink. Drain.

3. Stir in tomatoes, tomato paste, Italian seasoning, salt and pepper; cook 5 minutes.

4. Combine pasta, meat mixture and beans in prepared baking dish. Sprinkle with cheeses. Bake at 400°F for 20 to 30 minutes or until cheese is melted. Serve immediately.   *Makes 4 servings*

Note: This dish can be prepared a day in advance of baking and refrigerated, tightly covered with plastic wrap. If chilled, bake at 375°F for 35 to 45 minutes.

Prep Time: 30 minutes • Total Time: 50 to 60 minutes

Zucchini Lasagne

3 cans (8 ounces each) CONTADINA® Tomato Sauce
1 can (14.5 ounces) CONTADINA Stewed Tomatoes,
　　undrained
1 teaspoon granulated sugar
1 teaspoon Italian herb seasoning
1 teaspoon ground black pepper
1 pound lean ground beef
3 teaspoons seasoned salt
6 medium zucchini squash, sliced ⅛ inch thick
2 cups (8 ounces) shredded mozzarella cheese
2 cups (15 ounces) ricotta cheese
3 tablespoons grated Parmesan cheese

1. Combine tomato sauce, undrained stewed tomatoes, sugar, Italian seasoning and pepper in medium saucepan.

2. Simmer, uncovered, for 25 minutes, stirring occasionally. In medium skillet, brown beef; drain. Stir in seasoned salt and tomato sauce mixture.

3. Butter bottom of 13×9-inch baking dish. Layer half of zucchini slices on bottom of baking dish; sprinkle lightly with salt. Spoon half of ground beef mixture over zucchini. Sprinkle with mozzarella cheese; spread ricotta cheese evenly over mozzarella. Top with remaining zucchini slices; sprinkle lightly with salt. Spread with remaining beef mixture. Sprinkle Parmesan cheese on top.

4. Bake in preheated 350°F oven for 45 minutes.　　*Makes 8 servings*

Prep Time: 20 minutes • Cook Time: 70 minutes

Treasure Chest Casserole

  1 cup lentils, rinsed and drained
  1 can (16 ounces) whole tomatoes, cut up, drained
  1 potato, peeled and finely diced
  ½ cup chopped onion
  1 carrot, shredded
  Salt and black pepper to taste
  1 pound HILLSHIRE FARM® Polska Kielbasa, cut into
    1-inch-thick slices

Preheat oven to 350°F.

Combine lentils and 2 cups water in medium saucepan. Cook over medium-high heat until tender; drain, if necessary. Combine lentils, tomatoes, potato, onion, carrot, salt and pepper in small casserole. Top with Polska Kielbasa. Bake, covered, 45 minutes. Uncover; bake 15 minutes or until heated through. *Makes 4 to 6 servings*

Pizza Hot Dish

  1½ to 2 pounds ground beef
  ¼ cup chopped onion
  1 package (10 ounces) egg noodles
  2 jars (15½ ounces each) pizza sauce
  1 can (10¾ ounces) condensed Cheddar cheese soup
  2 cups (8 ounces) shredded mozzarella cheese

1. In large skillet brown ground beef with onion. Drain.

2. Prepare egg noodles according to package directions.

3. Add sauce, soup and cooked egg noodles to ground beef; mix well. Spoon into 13×9-inch baking pan or large casserole. Bake at 350°F for 30 minutes. Sprinkle with mozzarella cheese and bake an additional 15 minutes. *Makes 8 to 12 servings*

Favorite recipe from North Dakota Beef Commission

Meaty Meals

Johnny Marzetti

1 pound bulk mild Italian sausage
1 cup chopped onion
1 green bell pepper, chopped
1 clove garlic, minced
1 can (about 14 ounces) diced tomatoes, undrained
1 can (8 ounces) tomato sauce
1 can (6 ounces) tomato paste
1 cup water
1½ teaspoons Italian seasoning
½ teaspoon salt
⅛ teaspoon black pepper
1 package (12 ounces) wide egg noodles, cooked according to package directions and drained
2 cups (8 ounces) shredded mozzarella cheese
½ cup grated Parmesan cheese

1. Crumble sausage into 12-inch skillet. Cook and stir 2 minutes over medium heat. Add onion, bell pepper and garlic; cook and stir until onion is tender and sausage is no longer pink. Drain fat. Add tomatoes, tomato sauce, tomato paste, water, Italian seasoning, salt and pepper; cook and stir 8 to 10 minutes.

2. Meanwhile preheat oven to 375°F. Lightly spray 13×9-inch baking dish with nonstick cooking spray.

3. Place noodles in large bowl. Add sausage mixture; stir until well blended. Place half of noodle mixture into prepared baking dish. Sprinkle with half of mozzarella cheese. Repeat layers; sprinkle with Parmesan cheese. Bake 30 minutes or until heated through and cheese is melted.
Makes 6 servings

Tamale Pie

1 tablespoon BERTOLLI® Olive Oil
1 small onion, chopped
1 pound ground beef
1 envelope LIPTON® RECIPE SECRETS® Onion Soup Mix*
1 can (14½ ounces) stewed tomatoes, undrained
½ cup water
1 can (15 to 19 ounces) red kidney beans, rinsed and drained
1 package (8½ ounces) corn muffin mix

Also terrific with LIPTON® RECIPE SECRETS® Fiesta Herb with Red Pepper, Onion Mushroom, Beefy Onion or Beefy Mushroom Soup Mix.

1. Preheat oven to 400°F.

2. In 12-inch skillet, heat oil over medium heat and cook onion, stirring occasionally, 3 minutes or until tender. Stir in ground beef and cook until browned.

3. Stir in onion soup mix blended with tomatoes and water. Bring to a boil over high heat, stirring with spoon to crush tomatoes. Reduce heat to low and stir in beans. Simmer uncovered, stirring occasionally, 10 minutes. Turn into 2-quart casserole.

4. Prepare corn muffin mix according to package directions. Spoon evenly over casserole.

5. Bake uncovered 15 minutes or until corn topping is golden and filling is hot.   *Makes about 6 servings*

Italian Tomato Bake

1 pound sweet Italian sausage, cut into ½-inch slices
2 tablespoons butter
1 cup chopped onion
4 cups cooked egg noodles
2 cups frozen broccoli florets, thawed and drained
2 cups prepared pasta sauce
½ cup diced plum tomatoes
2 cloves garlic, minced
3 plum tomatoes, sliced
1 cup (8 ounces) ricotta cheese
⅓ cup grated Parmesan cheese
1 teaspoon dried oregano

1. Preheat oven to 350°F. Cook sausage in large skillet over medium heat about 10 minutes or until barely pink in center. Drain on paper towels; set aside. Drain fat from skillet.

2. Add butter and onion to skillet; cook and stir until onion is tender. Combine onion, noodles, broccoli, pasta sauce, diced tomatoes and garlic in large bowl; mix well. Transfer to 13×9-inch baking dish.

3. Top with cooked sausage and arrange tomato slices over top. Place 1 heaping tablespoonful ricotta cheese on each tomato slice. Sprinkle casserole with Parmesan cheese and oregano. Bake 35 minutes or until hot and bubbly. *Makes 6 servings*

When preparing pasta for a casserole,
reduce the cooking time by about one
third. The pasta will continue to cook
and absorb liquid during the baking time.

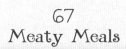
Meaty Meals

Pizza Casserole

1 pound BOB EVANS® Italian Roll Sausage
12 ounces wide noodles, cooked according to package
   directions
2 (14-ounce) jars pepperoni pizza sauce
2 cups (8 ounces) shredded Cheddar cheese
2 cups (8 ounces) shredded mozzarella cheese
6 ounces sliced pepperoni

Preheat oven to 350°F. Crumble and cook sausage in medium skillet over medium heat until browned. Drain on paper towels. Layer half of noodles in lightly greased 13×9-inch casserole dish. Top with half of sausage, half of pizza sauce, half of cheeses and half of pepperoni. Repeat layers with remaining ingredients, reserving several pepperoni slices for garnish on top of casserole. Bake 35 to 40 minutes. Refrigerate leftovers. *Makes 6 to 8 servings*

Creamy Beef and Vegetable Casserole

1 pound lean ground beef
1 small onion, chopped
1 bag (16 ounces) BIRDS EYE® frozen Farm Fresh Mixtures
   Broccoli, Corn & Red Peppers
1 can (10¾ ounces) cream of mushroom soup

• In medium skillet, brown beef and onion; drain excess fat.

• Meanwhile, in large saucepan, cook vegetables according to package directions; drain.

• Stir in beef mixture and soup. Cook over medium heat until heated through. *Makes 4 servings*

Serving Suggestion: Serve over rice and sprinkle with ½ cup shredded Cheddar cheese.

Prep Time: 5 minutes • Cook Time: 10 to 15 minutes

Tuscan Baked Rigatoni

1 pound Italian sausage, casings removed
1 pound rigatoni pasta, cooked, drained and kept warm
2 cups (8 ounces) shredded fontina cheese
2 tablespoons olive oil
2 fennel bulbs, thinly sliced
4 cloves garlic, minced
1 can (28 ounces) crushed tomatoes
1 cup heavy cream
1 teaspoon salt
1 teaspoon black pepper
8 cups coarsely chopped fresh spinach
1 can (15 ounces) cannellini beans, rinsed and drained
2 tablespoons pine nuts
½ cup grated Parmesan cheese

1. Preheat oven to 350°F. Spray 4-quart casserole with nonstick cooking spray. Crumble sausage in large skillet over medium-high heat. Cook and stir until no longer pink; drain. Transfer sausage to large bowl. Add pasta and fontina cheese; mix well.

2. Combine oil, fennel and garlic in same skillet. Cook and stir over medium heat 3 minutes or until fennel is tender. Add tomatoes, cream, salt and pepper; cook and stir until slightly thickened. Stir in spinach, beans and pine nuts; cook until heated through.

3. Pour tomato sauce mixture over pasta and sausage; toss to coat. Transfer to prepared casserole; sprinkle evenly with Parmesan cheese. Bake 30 minutes or until hot and bubbly.   *Makes 6 to 8 servings*

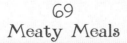

Family Favorite
Hamburger Casserole

1 tablespoon CRISCO® Oil* plus additional for oiling
1 cup chopped onion
1 pound ground beef round
1 package (9 ounces) frozen cut green beans
3 cups frozen southern style hash brown potatoes
1 can (10¾ ounces) zesty tomato soup
½ cup water
1 teaspoon dried basil leaves
¾ teaspoon salt
¼ teaspoon pepper
¼ cup plain dry bread crumbs

*Use your favorite Crisco Oil.

1. Heat oven to 350°F. Oil 11¾×7½×2-inch baking dish lightly. Place cooling rack on countertop.

2. Heat oil in large skillet on medium-high heat. Add onion. Cook and stir until tender. Add meat. Cook until browned, stirring occasionally. Add beans. Cook and stir 5 minutes or until thawed. Add potatoes.

3. Combine tomato soup and water in small bowl. Stir until well blended. Stir into skillet. Stir in basil, salt and pepper. Spoon into baking dish. Sprinkle with bread crumbs.

4. Bake at 350°F for 30 minutes or until potatoes are tender. *Do not overbake.* Let stand 5 minutes before serving.   *Makes 4 servings*

Quick Taco Macaroni & Cheese

1 package (12 ounces) large elbow macaroni (4 cups dried pasta)
1 tablespoon LAWRY'S® Seasoned Salt
1 pound lean ground beef or turkey
1 package (1 ounce) LAWRY'S® Taco Spices & Seasonings
2 cups (8 ounces) shredded Colby longhorn cheese
2 cups (8 ounces) shredded mild cheddar cheese
2 cups milk
3 eggs, beaten

In large stockpot, boil macaroni in unsalted water just until tender. Drain and toss with Seasoned Salt. Meanwhile in medium skillet, brown ground meat; drain fat. Stir in Taco Spices & Seasonings. Spray 13×9×2-inch baking dish with nonstick cooking spray. Layer half of macaroni in bottom of dish. Top with half of cheeses. Spread taco meat over top and repeat layers of macaroni and cheeses. In medium bowl, beat together milk and eggs. Pour egg mixture over top of casserole. Bake in preheated 350°F oven for 30 to 35 minutes or until golden brown.   *Makes 6 to 8 servings*

Variation: For spicier flavor, try using LAWRY'S® Chili Spices & Seasonings OR LAWRY'S® Hot Taco Spices & Seasonings instead of Taco Spices & Seasonings.

Prep Time: 20 to 22 minutes • Cook Time: 30 to 35 minutes

Sausage Tetrazzini

1 pound BOB EVANS® Italian Roll Sausage
1 medium onion, chopped
1 red or green bell pepper, chopped
½ pound spaghetti, cooked according to package directions
    and drained
1 (16-ounce) can stewed tomatoes, undrained
1 (10½-ounce) can condensed cream of mushroom soup
1 (10-ounce) can condensed tomato soup
½ pound fresh mushrooms, chopped
1 teaspoon minced garlic
½ teaspoon black pepper
    Salt to taste
1½ cups (6 ounces) shredded Cheddar cheese

Preheat oven to 350°F. Crumble sausage into large skillet. Cook over medium heat until lightly browned, stirring occasionally. Remove sausage; set aside. Add onion and red pepper to drippings in skillet; cook and stir until tender. Place in large bowl. Stir in spaghetti, tomatoes with juice, soups, mushrooms, garlic, black pepper, salt and reserved sausage; place in 3-quart casserole dish. Sprinkle with cheese; bake, uncovered, 30 to 35 minutes or until heated through. Serve hot. Refrigerate leftovers. *Makes 6 to 8 servings*

Easy Oven Beef Stew

2 pounds boneless beef stew meat, cut into 1½-inch cubes
1 can (16 ounces) tomatoes, undrained, cut up
1 can (10½ ounces) condensed beef broth
1 cup HOLLAND HOUSE® Red Cooking Wine
6 potatoes, peeled, quartered
6 carrots, cut into 2-inch pieces
3 ribs celery, cut into 1-inch pieces
2 medium onions, peeled, quartered
⅓ cup instant tapioca
1 tablespoon dried Italian seasoning*
¼ teaspoon black pepper
   Chopped fresh parsley

Or, substitute 1½ teaspoons each dried basil and oregano for Italian seasoning.

Heat oven to 325°F. Combine all ingredients except parsley in ovenproof Dutch oven; cover. Bake 2½ to 3 hours or until meat and vegetables are tender. Garnish with parsley.   *Makes 8 servings*

Monterey Black Bean Tortilla Supper

1 pound ground beef, browned and drained
1½ cups bottled salsa
1 (15-ounce) can black beans, drained
4 (8-inch) flour tortillas
2 cups (8 ounces) shredded Wisconsin Monterey Jack cheese*

For authentic Mexican flavor, substitute 2 cups shredded Wisconsin Queso Blanco.

Heat oven to 400°F. Combine ground beef, salsa and beans. In lightly greased 2-quart round casserole, layer one tortilla, ⅔ cup meat mixture and ½ cup cheese. Repeat layers three more times. Bake 30 minutes or until heated through.   *Makes 5 to 6 servings*

Favorite recipe from Wisconsin Milk Marketing Board

Tomato Pesto Lasagna

8 ounces lasagna noodles (2 inches wide)
1 pound crumbled sausage or ground beef
1 can (14½ ounces) DEL MONTE® Diced Tomatoes with
    Garlic & Onion
1 can (6 ounces) DEL MONTE Tomato Paste
8 ounces ricotta cheese
1 package (4 ounces) pesto sauce*
2 cups (8 ounces) shredded mozzarella cheese
    Grated Parmesan cheese (optional)

Pesto sauce is available frozen or refrigerated at the supermarket.

1. Cook noodles according to package directions; rinse, drain and separate noodles.

2. Meanwhile, brown meat in large skillet; drain. Stir in undrained tomatoes, tomato paste and ¾ cup water.

3. Layer ⅓ meat sauce, then half each of noodles, ricotta cheese, pesto and mozzarella cheese in 2-quart casserole or 9-inch square baking dish; repeat layers. Top with remaining meat sauce. Sprinkle with grated Parmesan cheese, if desired.

4. Bake at 350°F 30 minutes or until heated through.

Makes 6 servings

Microwave Directions: Assemble lasagna in 9-inch square microwavable dish as directed. Cover with vented plastic wrap; microwave on HIGH 10 minutes, rotating dish after 5 minutes.

Prep Time: 20 minutes • Cook Time: 30 minutes

Fix-It-Fast Corned Beef & Cabbage

1 small head cabbage (about 1½ pounds), cored and cut into 6 wedges
1 can (12 ounces) corned beef, sliced, *or* ½ pound sliced deli corned beef
1 can (16 ounces) sliced potatoes, drained
1 can (14 ounces) sliced carrots, drained
1⅓ cups *French's*® French Fried Onions, divided
1 can (10¾ ounces) condensed cream of celery soup
¾ cup water

Preheat oven to 375°F. Arrange cabbage wedges and corned beef slices alternately down center of 13×9-inch baking dish. Place potatoes, carrots and ⅔ *cup* French Fried Onions along sides of dish. In small bowl, combine soup and water; pour over meat and vegetables. Bake, covered, for 40 minutes or until cabbage is tender. Top with remaining ⅔ *cup* onions; bake, uncovered, 3 minutes or until onions are golden brown.   *Makes 4 to 6 servings*

Microwave Directions: Arrange cabbage wedges down center of 12×8-inch microwave-safe dish; add 2 tablespoons water. Cook, covered, on HIGH 10 to 12 minutes or until fork-tender. Rotate dish halfway through cooking time. Drain. Arrange cabbage, corned beef, potatoes, carrots and ⅔ *cup* onions in dish as above. Reduce water to ¼ cup. In small bowl, combine soup and water; pour over meat and vegetables. Cook, covered, 8 to 10 minutes or until vegetables are heated through. Rotate dish halfway through cooking time. Top with remaining ⅔ *cup* onions; cook, uncovered, 1 minute. Let stand 5 minutes.

Meaty Meals

Taco Salad Casserole

1 pound ground beef
1 cup chopped onion
1 can (15 ounces) chili with beans
1 can (14½ ounces) diced tomatoes, undrained
1 can (4 ounces) chopped green chilies, undrained
1 package (about 1 ounce) taco seasoning mix
1 bag (12 ounces) nacho-flavor tortilla chips, crushed and
    divided
2 cups (8 ounces) shredded Cheddar cheese
2 cups (8 ounces) shredded mozzarella cheese
3 to 4 cups shredded lettuce
1 jar (8 ounces) prepared taco sauce
½ cup sour cream

1. Preheat oven to 350°F.

2. Cook and stir beef and onion in large skillet over medium heat until meat is no longer pink; drain fat. Add chili with beans, tomatoes with juice, green chilies and taco seasoning; cook and stir until heated through.

3. Place half of crushed tortilla chips in 2½-quart casserole. Pour meat mixture over chips and top with cheeses and remaining chips. Bake 30 to 40 minutes or until hot and bubbly.

4. Serve over bed of lettuce; top with taco sauce and sour cream.

Makes 6 to 8 servings

Smoked Beef Casserole

1 jar (8 ounces) pasteurized processed cheese spread
¾ cup milk
2 packages (6 ounces each) HILLSHIRE FARM® Deli Select
**   Smoked Beef, cut into strips**
4 cups frozen hash brown potatoes, thawed
1 package (16 ounces) frozen peas
2 cups crushed potato chips, divided
½ cup (2 ounces) shredded Cheddar cheese

Preheat oven to 375°F.

Spoon cheese spread into 12×8-inch baking dish. Bake until cheese is melted. Stir milk into melted cheese. Mix in Smoked Beef, potatoes, peas and 1 cup potato chips. Bake, covered, 30 minutes. Top with Cheddar cheese and remaining 1 cup potato chips. Bake, uncovered, 3 minutes or until Cheddar cheese is melted.   *Makes 4 to 6 servings*

Swissed Ham and Noodles Casserole

2 tablespoons butter
½ cup chopped onion
½ cup chopped green pepper
1 can (10½ ounces) condensed cream of mushroom soup
1 cup dairy sour cream
1 package (8 ounces) medium noodles, cooked and drained
2 cups (8 ounces) shredded Wisconsin Swiss cheese
2 cups cubed cooked ham (about ¾ pound)

In 1-quart saucepan, melt butter; sauté onion and green pepper. Remove from heat; stir in soup and sour cream. In buttered 2-quart casserole, layer ⅓ of noodles, ⅓ of Swiss cheese, ⅓ of ham and ½ soup mixture. Repeat layers, ending with final ⅓ layer of noodles, cheese and ham. Bake in preheated 350°F oven 30 to 45 minutes or until heated through.
Makes 6 to 8 servings

Favorite recipe from Wisconsin Milk Marketing Board

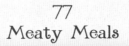

Cornmeal and Sausage Layered Dinner

1½ pounds **BOB EVANS® Italian Roll Sausage**
1 cup chopped onion
1 clove garlic, minced
1 (16-ounce) can diced tomatoes, undrained
1 (8-ounce) can tomato sauce
1 tablespoon chopped fresh basil *or* 1 teaspoon dried basil leaves
½ teaspoon ground black pepper
1½ cups yellow cornmeal
¾ teaspoon salt
3 cups water
1 cup grated Romano cheese

Crumble and cook sausage in large skillet until browned. Remove sausage from skillet and reserve. Pour off all but 1 tablespoon drippings. Add onion and garlic to skillet; cook until tender. Stir in tomatoes, tomato sauce, basil, pepper and sausage. Bring to a boil; reduce heat to low and simmer, uncovered, 25 minutes. Preheat oven to 375°F.

While sausage mixture is cooking, combine cornmeal, salt and water in medium saucepan. Bring to a boil, stirring constantly; cook and stir until thickened. Remove from heat; let cool slightly. Pour half of cornmeal mixture into greased 2½-quart casserole dish. Top with half of sausage mixture and sprinkle with half of cheese. Repeat with remaining cornmeal mixture, sausage mixture and cheese. Bake, uncovered, 30 minutes. Refrigerate leftovers.

Makes 6 servings

Corn Bread Taco Bake

1½ pounds ground beef
1 can (12 ounces) whole kernel corn, drained
1 can (8 ounces) tomato sauce
½ cup water
½ cup chopped green pepper
1 package (about 1⅛ ounces) taco seasoning mix
1 package (8½ ounces) corn muffin mix, plus ingredients to prepare mix
1⅓ cups *French's*® French Fried Onions, divided
½ cup (2 ounces) shredded Cheddar cheese

Preheat oven to 400°F. In large skillet, brown ground beef; drain. Stir in corn, tomato sauce, water, green pepper and taco seasoning; pour mixture into 2-quart casserole. In small bowl, prepare corn muffin mix according to package directions; stir in ⅔ *cup* French Fried Onions. Spoon corn muffin batter around edge of beef mixture. Bake, uncovered, at 400°F for 20 minutes or until corn bread is done. Top corn bread with cheese and remaining ⅔ *cup* onions; bake, uncovered, 1 to 3 minutes or until onions are golden brown. *Makes 6 servings*

Microwave Directions: Crumble ground beef into 12×8-inch microwave-safe dish. Cook, covered, on HIGH 4 to 6 minutes or until beef is cooked. Stir beef halfway through cooking time. Drain well. Prepare beef mixture and top with corn muffin batter as above. Cook, uncovered, on MEDIUM (50-60%) 7 to 9 minutes or until corn bread is nearly done. Rotate dish halfway through cooking time. Top corn bread with cheese and remaining ⅔ *cup* onions; cook, uncovered, on HIGH 1 minute or until cheese melts. Cover casserole and let stand 10 minutes. (Corn bread will finish baking during standing time.)

Michigan Goulash

2 tablespoons vegetable oil
1 pound lean ground beef or ground turkey
1 medium onion, chopped
1 large green bell pepper, seeded and diced
3 ribs celery, cut into thin slices
1 small zucchini, cut into thin slices
1 jalapeño pepper,* seeded and minced
1 can (8 ounces) tomato sauce
1 cup water
¾ cup barbecue sauce
1 package (8 to 10 ounces) egg noodles, cooked and
    kept warm
2 cups (8 ounces) shredded Cheddar cheese

Jalapeño peppers can sting and irritate the skin; wear rubber gloves when handling peppers and do not touch eyes. Wash hands after handling peppers.

1. Preheat oven to 350°F. Grease 13×9-inch baking dish.

2. Heat oil in large skillet over medium-high heat. Add beef, stirring to break up meat. Add onion, bell pepper, celery, zucchini and jalapeño pepper; cook and stir until meat is no longer pink. Add tomato sauce, water and barbecue sauce; stir to combine. Reduce heat to medium-low and simmer 20 minutes.

3. Combine meat mixture and noodles in prepared dish; top with cheese.

4. Bake 10 to 15 minutes or until cheese is melted.

Makes 8 servings

Ortega® Fiesta Bake

1 pound ground beef
1 cup chopped onion
¾ cup ORTEGA® Salsa-Thick & Chunky
1 package (1¼ ounces) ORTEGA Taco Seasoning Mix
¼ cup water
1 cup whole-kernel corn
1 can (2¼ ounces) sliced ripe olives, drained
1 package (8½ ounces) corn muffin mix
1 cup (4 ounces) shredded cheddar cheese
1 can (4 ounces) ORTEGA Diced Green Chiles

PREHEAT oven to 350°F.

COOK beef and onion until beef is browned; drain. Stir in salsa, seasoning mix and water. Cook over low heat for 5 to 6 minutes or until mixture thickens. Stir in corn and olives. Spoon into 8-inch-square baking dish.

PREPARE batter for corn muffin mix according to package directions. Stir in cheese and chiles. Spread over meat mixture.

BAKE for 30 to 35 minutes or until crust is golden brown.

Makes 6 servings

Ground beef and other meats
should be the last items to go in your
shopping cart at the supermarket, and
the first to go in the refrigerator when
you return home. This will prevent
the meat from spending too much
time at unsafe temperatures.

Sausage and Cheese Potato Casserole

  1 pound BOB EVANS® Italian Roll Sausage
  4 cups cubed unpeeled red skin potatoes
  1 cup (4 ounces) shredded Monterey Jack cheese
  ¼ cup chopped green onions
  1 (4-ounce) can chopped green chiles, drained
  6 eggs
  ¾ cup milk
  ¼ teaspoon salt
  ⅛ teaspoon black pepper
  ½ cup grated Parmesan cheese

Preheat oven to 350°F. Crumble and cook sausage in skillet until browned. Drain off drippings. Spread potatoes in greased 13×9-inch baking pan. Top with cooked sausage, Monterey Jack cheese, green onions and chiles. Whisk eggs, milk, salt and pepper until frothy. Pour egg mixture over sausage layer; bake 30 minutes. Remove from oven. Sprinkle with Parmesan cheese; bake 15 minutes more or until eggs are set. Refrigerate leftovers. *Makes 6 to 8 servings*

Pork Chop & Wild Rice Bake

  1 package (6 ounces) seasoned long grain & wild rice mix
  2 cups water
  1⅓ cups *French's®* French Fried Onions, divided
  1 package (10 ounces) frozen cut green beans, thawed,
    drained
  ¼ cup orange juice
  1 teaspoon grated orange peel
  4 boneless pork chops (1 inch thick)

1. Preheat oven to 375°F. Combine rice mix and seasoning packet, water, ⅔ *cup* French Fried Onions, green beans, orange juice and orange peel in 2-quart shallow baking dish. Arrange pork chops on top.

2. Bake, uncovered, 30 minutes or until pork chops are no longer pink near center. Sprinkle chops with remaining ⅔ *cup* onions. Bake 5 minutes or until onions are golden. *Makes 4 servings*

Oven-Baked Black Bean Chili

1½ pounds ground beef
¼ cup chopped onion
¼ cup chopped green bell pepper
1 can (about 15 ounces) black beans, rinsed and drained
1 can (14½ ounces) diced tomatoes with green chilies
1 can (about 14 ounces) beef broth
1 can (8 ounces) tomato sauce
5 tablespoons chili powder
1 tablespoon sugar
1 tablespoon ground cumin
1 teaspoon dried minced onion
⅛ teaspoon garlic powder
⅛ teaspoon ground ginger
2 cups (8 ounces) Mexican-blend shredded cheese

1. Preheat oven to 350°F. Cook and stir beef, onion and bell pepper in large skillet over medium-high heat until meat is no longer pink. Drain and transfer to 4-quart casserole.

2. Add remaining ingredients except cheese; stir until well blended. Cover and bake 30 minutes, stirring every 10 minutes. Uncover and top with cheese. Bake 5 minutes or until cheese melts.

Makes 6 to 8 servings

Serving Suggestion: Serve with Mexican-style cornbread.

Meaty Meals

Hamburger Casserole Ole

1 pound lean ground beef or ground turkey
1 package (1¼ ounces) taco seasoning mix
1 cup water
1 box (9 ounces) BIRDS EYE® frozen Cut Green Beans
½ cup shredded sharp Cheddar cheese
½ cup shredded mozzarella cheese

• Preheat oven to 325°F.

• Brown beef; drain excess fat. Add taco mix and water; cook over low heat 8 to 10 minutes or until liquid has been absorbed.

• Meanwhile, cook green beans according to package directions; drain.

• Spread meat in greased 13×9-inch baking pan. Spread beans over meat. Sprinkle with cheeses.

• Bake 15 to 20 minutes or until hot and cheese is melted.

Makes 4 servings

Serving Suggestion: Serve over tortillas or corn chips and top with sour cream, chopped avocado, chopped lettuce and/or chopped tomatoes.

Birds Eye Idea: Try substituting plain low-fat yogurt for sour cream in your recipes for a lighter version.

Prep Time: 15 minutes • Cook Time: 25 to 30 minutes

Meatball Stroganoff

1 can (10¾ ounces) condensed cream of mushroom soup, undiluted
1 container (8 ounces) sour cream
1 cup milk
1 package (15 ounces) frozen prepared meatballs, thawed and cut in half if large
4 cups cooked egg noodles (5 ounces uncooked)
1 cup (4 ounces) shredded Swiss cheese
2 cups *French's*® French Fried Onions, divided
¼ cup minced fresh parsley
1 tablespoon *French's*® Worcestershire Sauce
1 teaspoon paprika

1. Preheat oven to 350°F. Coat 3-quart shallow baking dish with vegetable cooking spray.

2. Combine soup, sour cream and milk in large bowl. Stir in meatballs, noodles, cheese, *1 cup* French Fried Onions, parsley, Worcestershire and paprika. Spoon into prepared baking dish.

3. Bake 25 minutes or until heated through. Stir. Sprinkle with remaining *1 cup* onions; bake 5 minutes or until onions are golden brown.   *Makes 4 servings*

Prep Time: **10 minutes** • Cook Time: **30 minutes**

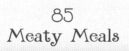

Summer Fiesta Casserole

2 pounds ground beef
1 medium onion, chopped
1 package (about 1 ounce) taco seasoning mix
4 to 6 potatoes, peeled and cut into ½-inch cubes
(about 4 cups)
1 to 2 tablespoons vegetable oil
4 cups sliced zucchini
1 can (14½ ounces) diced tomatoes with onion and garlic,
undrained
1½ cups (6 ounces) shredded Mexican cheese blend

1. Preheat oven to 350°F. Spray 4-quart casserole with nonstick cooking spray.

2. Cook beef and onion in large skillet over medium heat until meat is no longer pink, stirring to separate meat; drain fat. Add taco seasoning; cook 5 minutes, stirring occasionally. Transfer meat mixture to prepared casserole.

3. Add potatoes to same skillet; cook and stir over medium heat until potatoes are browned, adding oil as needed to prevent sticking. Add zucchini; cook and stir until beginning to soften. Transfer to casserole; top with tomatoes and cheese.

4. Bake 10 to 15 minutes or until cheese is melted and casserole is heated through. *Makes 4 to 6 servings*

Serving Suggestion: Serve with tortilla chips, sour cream and salsa.

Family-Style Frankfurters with Rice and Red Beans

1 tablespoon vegetable oil
1 medium onion, chopped
½ medium green bell pepper, chopped
2 cloves garlic, minced
1 can (14 ounces) red kidney beans, rinsed and drained
1 can (14 ounces) Great Northern beans, rinsed and drained
½ pound beef frankfurters, cut into ¼-inch-thick pieces
1 cup uncooked instant brown rice
1 cup vegetable broth
¼ cup packed brown sugar
¼ cup ketchup
3 tablespoons dark molasses
1 tablespoon Dijon mustard

1. Preheat oven to 350°F. Spray 13×9-inch baking dish with nonstick cooking spray.

2. Heat oil in Dutch oven over medium-high heat until hot. Add onion, bell pepper and garlic; cook and stir 2 minutes or until onion is tender.

3. Add beans, frankfurters, rice, broth, brown sugar, ketchup, molasses and mustard to vegetables; stir to blend. Transfer to prepared dish.

4. Cover tightly with foil and bake 30 minutes or until rice is tender.

Makes 6 servings

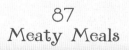

Oven Jambalaya

1 pound sweet Italian sausage
2 stalks celery, sliced
1 green bell pepper, diced
1 medium onion, diced
2 cloves garlic, minced
1 (28-ounce) can crushed tomatoes
2 cups chicken broth
1 cup long-grain rice
2 teaspoons TABASCO® brand Pepper Sauce
1 teaspoon salt
1 pound large shrimp, peeled and deveined

Preheat oven to 400°F. Cook sausage in 12-inch skillet over medium-high heat until well browned on all sides, turning frequently. Remove sausage to plate; reserve drippings in skillet. When cool enough to handle, cut sausage into ½-inch slices. Add celery, green bell pepper, onion and garlic to same skillet; cook 3 minutes over medium heat, stirring occasionally.

Combine tomatoes, chicken broth, rice, TABASCO® Sauce, salt, sausage and vegetable mixture in 3-quart casserole. Bake 40 minutes. Stir in shrimp; cook 5 minutes or until rice is tender and shrimp are cooked. *Makes 8 servings*

Meaty Meals

Speedy Sirloin Steak Casserole

1 (1½-pound) beef top sirloin steak, cut 1 inch thick
2 tablespoons Lucini Premium Select extra virgin olive oil, divided
1 sheet refrigerated pie dough
1 teaspoon dried dill weed
½ teaspoon salt
1 medium onion, coarsely chopped
½ pound mushrooms, cut into quarters
1 tablespoon all-purpose flour
½ cup milk
1 teaspoon ground nutmeg
1 teaspoon beef bouillon granules
8 ounces (2 cups) shredded JARLSBERG cheese
2 cups frozen peas

Cut beef into ¼-inch-thick slices. Cut each slice into 1-inch pieces. Combine with 1 tablespoon oil. Allow pie dough to stand at room temperature as package directs.

Heat large nonstick skillet until hot. Stir-fry beef mixture (half at a time) 1 to 2 minutes. Remove from skillet. Combine beef mixture, dill and salt; set aside.

Heat remaining 1 tablespoon oil in same skillet; add onion and cook until softened, about 3 to 4 minutes. Add mushrooms; cook 5 minutes, stirring frequently. Sprinkle with flour; cook 1 minute. Add milk, nutmeg and bouillon. Bring mixture to a boil and cook, stirring constantly, until mixture thickens. Add cheese; mix lightly until cheese melts. Stir in reserved beef mixture with accumulated juices and peas.

Spoon mixture into round 2-quart casserole. Fold pie crust edges under to fit inside edge of casserole; place on top of meat mixture. Crimp edges decoratively and cut slits in several places near center (to prevent "cracking"). Bake casserole in preheated 450°F oven 10 to 12 minutes or until crust is browned. *Makes 6 servings*

Prep Time: 30 minutes • Cook Time: 10 to 12 minutes

Mediterranean-Style Tuna Noodle Casserole

1 tablespoon Lucini Premium Select extra virgin
  olive oil
4 cloves garlic, minced
2 large onions, chopped (1½ cups)
12 ounces mushrooms, chopped (4 cups)
2 large tomatoes, chopped
1 red bell pepper, diced (1 cup)
1 green bell pepper, diced (1 cup)
1 cup chopped fresh cilantro leaves *or* ¼ cup dried
  oregano leaves
2 tablespoons dried marjoram or oregano leaves
1 to 2 teaspoons ground red pepper
1 pound JARLSBERG LITE™ cheese, shredded (4 cups)
1 (16-ounce) can black-eyed peas, rinsed and drained
2 (7-ounce) cans tuna, drained and flaked
6 ounces cooked pasta (tricolor rotelle, bows or
  macaroni)

Preheat oven to 350°F. Heat oil in large skillet; sauté garlic
until golden. Add onions; sauté over medium-high heat
about 2 minutes or until transparent.

Add mushrooms, tomatoes and bell peppers; cook and
stir 3 to 5 minutes or until mushrooms begin to brown.
Add cilantro, marjoram and ground red pepper.

Toss with cheese, peas, tuna and pasta. Pour into greased
baking dish. Bake, covered, 45 minutes or until cooked
through.   *Makes 6 to 8 servings*

Sicilian Fish and Rice Bake

3 tablespoons olive or vegetable oil
¾ cup chopped onion
½ cup chopped celery
1 clove garlic, minced
½ cup uncooked long-grain white rice
2 cans (14.5 ounces each) CONTADINA® Recipe Ready
    Diced Tomatoes, undrained
1 teaspoon salt
1 teaspoon ground black pepper
½ teaspoon granulated sugar
⅛ teaspoon cayenne pepper
1 pound firm white fish
¼ cup finely chopped fresh parsley

1. Heat oil in large skillet. Add onion, celery and garlic; sauté for 2 to 3 minutes or until vegetables are tender.

2. Stir in rice; sauté for 5 minutes or until rice browns slightly. Add undrained tomatoes, salt, black pepper, sugar and cayenne pepper; mix well.

3. Place fish in bottom of greased 12×7½-inch baking dish. Spoon rice mixture over fish; cover with foil.

4. Bake in preheated 400°F oven for 45 to 50 minutes or until rice is tender. Let stand for 5 minutes before serving. Sprinkle with parsley.

Makes 6 servings

Prep Time: 6 minutes • Cook Time: 58 minutes

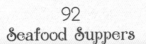

Louisiana Seafood Bake

1 can (14½ ounces) whole tomatoes, undrained and cut up
1 can (8 ounces) tomato sauce
1 cup water
1 cup sliced celery
1⅓ cups *French's*® French Fried Onions, divided
⅔ cup uncooked regular rice
1 teaspoon *Frank's*® *RedHot*® Original Cayenne Pepper Sauce
½ teaspoon garlic powder
¼ teaspoon dried oregano, crushed
¼ teaspoon dried thyme, crushed
½ pound white fish, thawed if frozen and cut into 1-inch chunks
1 can (4 ounces) shrimp, drained
⅓ cup sliced pitted ripe olives
¼ cup (1 ounce) grated Parmesan cheese

Preheat oven to 375°F. In 1½-quart casserole, combine tomatoes, tomato sauce, water, celery, ⅔ *cup* French Fried Onions, uncooked rice and seasonings. Bake, covered, at 375°F for 20 minutes. Stir in fish, shrimp and olives. Bake, covered, 20 minutes or until heated through. Top with cheese and remaining ⅔ *cup* onions; bake, uncovered, 3 minutes or until onions are golden brown.

Makes 4 servings

Microwave Directions: In 2-quart microwave-safe casserole, prepare rice mixture as above. Cook, covered, on HIGH 15 minutes, stirring rice halfway through cooking time. Add fish, shrimp and olives. Cook, covered, 12 to 14 minutes or until rice is cooked. Stir casserole halfway through cooking time. Top with cheese and remaining ⅔ *cup* onions; cook, uncovered, 1 minute. Let stand 5 minutes.

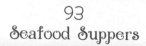

Tuna Vegetable Medley

8 ounces cooked egg noodles
1 package (10 ounces) frozen chopped broccoli, thawed and
    well drained
1 package (10 ounces) frozen carrots, thawed and well drained
1 can (10¾ ounces) cream of mushroom soup
1 cup corn
1 (7-ounce) STARKIST Flavor Fresh Pouch® Tuna
    (Albacore or Chunk Light)
1 cup shredded Swiss, Cheddar or Monterey Jack Cheese
⅔ cup milk
    Salt and pepper to taste
¼ cup grated Parmesan cheese

In large bowl, combine all ingredients except Parmesan cheese; mix well. Pour mixture into 2-quart baking dish; top with Parmesan cheese. Bake in 400°F oven 20 to 30 minutes or until thoroughly heated and golden on top. *Makes 6 servings*

Prep Time: 40 minutes

Fish a la Paolo

1 (16-ounce) jar NEWMAN'S OWN® Medium Salsa
1 (10-ounce) package frozen chopped spinach, thawed,
    drained and squeezed dry (or favorite mild vegetable)
2 tablespoons capers
1 tablespoon lemon juice
1 pound firm fresh fish, such as scrod fillets, cut into 4 pieces
1 tablespoon butter, cut into small pieces
1 large tomato, thinly sliced
½ cup fresh cilantro leaves, chopped

Preheat oven to 400°F. Mix salsa with spinach, capers and lemon juice; place in bottom of 11×7-inch baking dish. Place fish on top. Dot fish with butter and top with tomato slices.

Bake 25 minutes. Remove from oven and top with chopped cilantro.
Makes 4 servings

Scallop and Artichoke Heart Casserole

1 package (9 ounces) frozen artichoke hearts, cooked and
   drained
1 pound scallops
1 teaspoon canola or vegetable oil
¼ cup chopped red bell pepper
¼ cup sliced green onion tops
¼ cup all-purpose flour
2 cups milk
1 teaspoon dried tarragon
¼ teaspoon salt
¼ teaspoon white pepper
1 tablespoon chopped fresh parsley
   Dash paprika

1. Cut large artichoke hearts lengthwise into halves. Arrange artichoke hearts in even layer in 8-inch square baking dish.

2. Rinse scallops; pat dry with paper towel. If scallops are large, cut into halves. Arrange scallops evenly over artichokes.

3. Preheat oven to 350°F. Heat oil in medium saucepan over medium-low heat. Add bell pepper and green onions; cook and stir 5 minutes or until tender. Stir in flour. Gradually stir in milk until smooth. Add tarragon, salt and white pepper; cook and stir over medium heat 10 minutes or until sauce boils and thickens.

4. Pour sauce over scallops. Bake, uncovered, 25 minutes or until bubbling and scallops are opaque. Sprinkle with parsley and paprika before serving.

Makes 4 servings

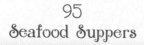

Sole Almondine

1 package (6.5 ounces) RICE-A-RONI® Broccoli Au Gratin
1 medium zucchini
4 sole, scrod or orange roughy fillets
1 tablespoon lemon juice
¼ cup grated Parmesan cheese, divided
Salt and pepper (optional)
¼ cup sliced almonds
2 tablespoons margarine or butter, melted

1. Prepare Rice-A-Roni® Mix as package directs.

2. Meanwhile, cut zucchini lengthwise into 12 thin strips. Heat oven to 350°F.

3. In 11×7-inch glass baking dish, spread prepared rice evenly. Set aside. Sprinkle fish with lemon juice, 2 tablespoons cheese, salt and pepper, if desired. Place zucchini strips over fish; roll up. Place fish seam-side down on rice.

4. Combine almonds and margarine; sprinkle evenly over fish. Top with remaining 2 tablespoons cheese. Bake 20 to 25 minutes or until fish flakes easily with fork. *Makes 4 servings*

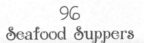
Tip

Choose zucchini that are heavy for
their size, firm and well shaped.
They should have a bright color and
be free of cuts and any soft spots.

Herb-Baked Fish & Rice

1½ cups hot chicken broth
½ cup uncooked white rice
¼ teaspoon Italian seasoning
¼ teaspoon garlic powder
1 package (10 ounces) frozen chopped broccoli, thawed and
   drained
1⅓ cups *French's®* French Fried Onions, divided
1 tablespoon grated Parmesan cheese
1 pound unbreaded fish fillets, thawed if frozen
   Paprika (optional)
½ cup (2 ounces) shredded Cheddar cheese

Preheat oven to 375°F. In 12×8-inch baking dish, combine broth,
uncooked rice and seasonings. Bake, covered, at 375°F for 10 minutes.
Top with broccoli, ⅔ *cup* French Fried Onions and Parmesan cheese.
Place fish fillets diagonally down center of dish; sprinkle fish lightly
with paprika. Bake, covered, at 375°F for 20 to 25 minutes or until
fish flakes easily with fork. Stir rice. Top fish with Cheddar cheese
and remaining ⅔ *cup* French Fried Onions; bake, uncovered, 3 minutes
or until onions are golden brown.   *Makes 3 to 4 servings*

Microwave Directions: In 12×8-inch microwave-safe dish, prepare rice
mixture as above, except reduce broth to 1¼ cups. Cook, covered, on
HIGH 5 minutes, stirring halfway through cooking time. Stir in broccoli,
⅔ *cup* onions and Parmesan cheese. Arrange fish fillets in single layer on
top of rice mixture; sprinkle fish lightly with paprika. Cook, covered, on
MEDIUM (50 to 60%) 18 to 20 minutes or until fish flakes easily with
fork and rice is done. (Rotate dish halfway through cooking time.) Top
fish with Cheddar cheese and remaining ⅔ *cup* onions; cook, uncovered,
on HIGH 1 minute or until cheese melts. Let stand 5 minutes.

Seafood Alfredo Pot Pie

1 cup chopped onion
1 tablespoon extra-virgin olive oil
2 cups heavy whipping cream
2 cups shredded Parmesan cheese
2 tablespoons cornstarch
½ pound sea scallops, quartered
½ pound large cooked shrimp, peeled and deveined
½ pound imitation crabmeat, flaked
1 can (15 ounces) VEG•ALL® Original Mixed Vegetables, drained
1 tablespoon chopped fresh parsley
1 package (10 ounces) refrigerated pizza dough

Preheat oven to 400°F.

In large saucepan, sauté onion in oil over medium heat until softened. Add cream and bring to a boil.

Combine cheese and cornstarch. Add to cream; cook and stir until thickened.

Remove from heat; stir in seafood, Veg•All and parsley. Transfer to greased 13×9-inch baking dish.

Unroll pizza dough and place on top of seafood mixture. Bake for 15 to 20 minutes or until top is golden brown.

Makes 4 to 6 servings

Prep time: 20 minutes

Albacore Quiche

1 (9-inch) pie shell or 1 refrigerated (½ of 15-ounce package) pie crust
1 (3-ounce) STARKIST Flavor Fresh Pouch® Tuna (Albacore)
⅓ cup chopped green onions
¾ cup shredded Cheddar or Swiss cheese or a combination of cheeses
3 large eggs
1¼ cups half-and-half or milk
½ teaspoon dried basil or dill weed
¼ teaspoon ground black pepper

Line pie shell with foil; fill with pie weights, dry beans or rice. Bake in 375°F oven 10 minutes. Remove foil and pie weights; place tuna, onions and cheese in pie shell. In medium bowl, combine eggs, half-and-half and seasonings; pour into pie shell. Continue baking 40 to 50 minutes more or until quiche is set and knife inserted near center comes out clean. Cool slightly before serving.

Makes 6 servings

So-Easy Fish Divan

1 package (about 1⅛ ounces) cheese sauce mix
1⅓ cups milk
1 bag (16 ounces) frozen vegetable combination (brussels sprouts, carrots, cauliflower), thawed and drained
1⅓ cups *French's*® French Fried Onions, divided
1 pound unbreaded fish fillets, thawed if frozen
½ cup (2 ounces) shredded Cheddar cheese

Preheat oven to 375°F. In small saucepan, prepare cheese sauce according to package directions using 1⅓ cups milk. In 12×8-inch baking dish, combine vegetables and ⅔ *cup* French Fried Onions; top with fish fillets. Pour cheese sauce over fish and vegetables. Bake, covered, 25 minutes or until fish flakes easily with fork. Top fish with Cheddar cheese and remaining ⅔ *cup* onions; bake, uncovered, 3 minutes or until onions are golden brown.

Makes 3 to 4 servings

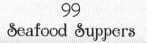

Baked Fish Galician Style

½ cup plus 4 teaspoons **FILIPPO BERIO®** Olive Oil, divided
1 large onion, chopped
2 tablespoons minced fresh parsley, divided
2 cloves garlic, crushed
2 teaspoons paprika
1½ pounds new potatoes, peeled and cut into ⅛-inch-thick
    slices
1 tablespoon all-purpose flour
3 small bay leaves
½ teaspoon dried thyme leaves
    Dash ground cloves
4 orange roughy or scrod fillets, 1 inch thick (about 2 pounds)
    Salt and freshly ground black pepper
    Lemon wedges (optional)

Preheat oven to 350°F. In large skillet, heat ½ cup olive oil over medium heat until hot. Add onion; cook and stir 5 to 7 minutes or until softened. Stir in 1 tablespoon parsley, garlic and paprika. Add potatoes; stir until lightly coated with mixture. Sprinkle with flour. Add enough water to cover potatoes; stir gently to blend. Add bay leaves, thyme and cloves. Bring to a boil. Cover; reduce heat to low and simmer 20 to 25 minutes or until potatoes are just tender. *(Do not overcook potatoes.)*

Spoon potato mixture into 1 large or 2 small casseroles. Place fish fillets on top of potato mixture. Drizzle 1 teaspoon of remaining olive oil over each fillet. Spoon sauce from bottom of casserole over each fillet.

Bake 15 to 20 minutes or until fish flakes easily when tested with fork. Sprinkle fillets with remaining 1 tablespoon parsley. Season to taste with salt and pepper. Remove bay leaves before serving. Serve with lemon wedges, if desired. *Makes 4 servings*

Salmon & Noodle Casserole

6 ounces uncooked wide noodles
1 teaspoon vegetable oil
1 medium onion, finely chopped
¾ cup thinly sliced carrot
¾ cup thinly sliced celery
1 can (about 15 ounces) salmon, drained, skin and bones
    discarded
1 can (10¾ ounces) cream of celery soup, undiluted
1 cup (4 ounces) shredded Cheddar cheese
¾ cup frozen peas
½ cup sour cream
¼ cup milk
⅛ teaspoon dried dill weed
    Black pepper

1. Preheat oven to 350°F. Cook noodles in large saucepan according to package directions; drain and return to saucepan.

2. Meanwhile, heat oil in large skillet over medium heat. Add onion, carrot and celery; cook and stir 4 to 5 minutes or until carrot is crisp-tender.

3. Add salmon, onion mixture, soup, cheese, peas, sour cream, milk, dill weed and pepper to noodles; stir gently until blended. Pour into 2-quart casserole dish. Cover and bake 25 to 30 minutes or until hot and bubbly.   *Makes 4 to 5 servings*

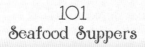

Crunchy Tuna Squares

1 (7-ounce) STARKIST Flavor Fresh Pouch® Tuna (Albacore)
1 cup chopped celery
1 cup chopped roasted cashews
½ cup drained sliced water chestnuts
½ cup chopped green onions, including tops
⅓ cup chopped drained roasted red peppers
1½ cups shredded Cheddar cheese, divided
½ cup mayonnaise or light mayonnaise
½ cup sour cream or light sour cream
2 tablespoons lemon juice
¾ teaspoon seasoned salt
1 cup cheese crackers, crushed into coarse crumbs

In medium bowl, place tuna, celery, cashews, water chestnuts, onions, peppers and 1 cup cheese; mix lightly with fork. In small bowl, whisk together mayonnaise, sour cream, lemon juice and seasoned salt. Add to tuna mixture; mix gently.

Spoon into greased 11×7-inch baking pan. Sprinkle with crushed cracker crumbs; top with remaining ½ cup cheese. Bake in 450°F oven 12 to 15 minutes or until mixture bubbles and begins to brown. Let stand several minutes before cutting into 6 squares.

Makes 6 servings

Prep Time: 20 minutes

To crush crackers easily, place them in a
large resealable food storage bag. Seal the
bag, then roll over the crackers with
a rolling pin or crush them with a meat
mallet or the bottom of a glass.

Creamy Alfredo Seafood Lasagna

1 jar (1 pound) RAGÚ® Cheesy!® Classic Alfredo Sauce,
    divided
1 pound imitation crabmeat, separated into bite-sized pieces
1 container (15 ounces) ricotta cheese
2 cups shredded mozzarella cheese (about 8 ounces), divided
1 small onion, chopped
12 lasagna noodles, cooked and drained
2 tablespoons grated Parmesan cheese

1. Preheat oven to 350°F. In medium bowl, combine ½ cup Ragú
Alfredo Sauce, crabmeat, ricotta cheese, 1½ cups mozzarella
cheese and onion; set aside.

2. In 13×9-inch baking dish, spread ½ cup Alfredo Sauce. Arrange
4 lasagna noodles, then top with ½ of ricotta mixture. Repeat
layers, ending with noodles. Top with remaining ½ cup sauce.

3. Cover with aluminum foil and bake 40 minutes. Remove foil
and sprinkle with remaining ½ cup mozzarella cheese and Parmesan
cheese. Bake an additional 10 minutes or until cheeses are melted. Let
stand 10 minutes before serving.   *Makes 8 servings*

Prep Time: 25 minutes • Cook Time: 50 minutes

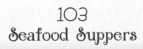

Baja Fish and Rice Bake

 3 tablespoons vegetable oil
¾ cup chopped onion
½ cup chopped celery
 1 clove garlic, minced
½ cup uncooked white rice
 2 cans (14.5 ounces each) CONTADINA® Stewed Tomatoes,
   cut up, undrained
 1 teaspoon lemon pepper seasoning
½ teaspoon salt
⅛ teaspoon cayenne pepper
 1 pound fish fillets (any firm white fish)
¼ cup finely chopped fresh parsley
   Lemon slices (optional)

1. Heat oil in large skillet over medium heat; sauté onion, celery and garlic.

2. Stir in rice; sauté about 5 minutes or until rice browns slightly. Add undrained tomatoes, lemon pepper, salt and cayenne pepper.

3. Place fish fillets in bottom of 12×7½×2-inch baking dish. Spoon rice mixture over fish.

4. Cover with foil; bake in preheated 400°F oven for 45 to 50 minutes or until rice is tender. Allow to stand 5 minutes before serving. Sprinkle with parsley. Garnish with lemon slices, if desired. *Makes 6 servings*

Prep Time: 8 minutes • Cook Time: 58 minutes

Microwave Directions: Combine onion, celery and garlic in microwave-safe bowl. Microwave on HIGH (100%) for 3 minutes. Stir in rice, tomatoes and juice, lemon pepper, salt and cayenne pepper. Microwave on HIGH for an additional 5 minutes. Place fish fillets in 12×7½×2-inch microwave-safe baking dish. Spoon rice mixture over fish. Cover tightly with plastic wrap, turning up corner to vent. Microwave on HIGH for 20 to 25 minutes or until rice is tender. Allow to stand 5 minutes before serving. Serve as above.

Seafood Pasta

½ cup olive oil
1 pound asparagus, cut into 1-inch pieces
1 cup chopped green onions
5 teaspoons chopped garlic
1 package (about 16 ounces) linguine, cooked and drained
1 pound medium shrimp, shelled, deveined and cooked
1 package (8 ounces) imitation crabmeat
1 package (8 ounces) imitation lobster
1 can (8 ounces) sliced black olives, drained

1. Preheat oven to 350°F. Spray 4-quart casserole with nonstick cooking spray. Heat oil in large skillet over medium heat. Add asparagus, green onions and garlic; cook and stir until tender.

2. Combine asparagus mixture, linguine, seafood and olives in prepared casserole. Bake 30 minutes or until heated through.   *Makes 6 servings*

Chesapeake Crab Strata

¼ cup butter or margarine
4 cups unseasoned croutons
2 cups (8 ounces) shredded Cheddar cheese
2 cups milk
8 eggs, beaten
½ teaspoon dry mustard
½ teaspoon seafood seasoning
  Salt and black pepper
1 pound crabmeat, picked over to remove any shells

1. Preheat oven to 325°F. Place butter in 11×7-inch baking dish. Heat in oven until melted, tilting to coat dish. Remove dish from oven; spread croutons over melted butter. Top with cheese; set aside.

2. Combine milk, eggs, mustard, seafood seasoning, salt and pepper; mix well. Pour egg mixture over cheese in dish; sprinkle with crabmeat. Bake 50 minutes or until mixture is set. Remove from oven and let stand about 10 minutes.   *Makes 6 to 8 servings*

Biscuit-Topped Tuna Bake

 2 tablespoons vegetable oil
½ cup chopped onion
½ cup chopped celery
 1 can (10¾ ounces) condensed cream of potato soup
 1 package (10 ounces) frozen peas and carrots, thawed
 1 (7-ounce) STARKIST Flavor Fresh Pouch® Tuna
     (Albacore or Chunk Light)
¾ cup milk
¼ teaspoon garlic powder
¼ teaspoon ground black pepper
 1 can (7½ ounces) refrigerator flaky biscuits

In large skillet, heat oil over medium-high heat; sauté onion and celery until onion is soft. Add remaining ingredients except biscuits; heat thoroughly. Transfer mixture to 1½-quart casserole. Arrange biscuits around top edge of dish; bake in 400°F oven 10 to 15 minutes or until biscuits are golden brown. *Makes 4 to 6 servings*

Prep and Cook Time: 25 minutes

Crunchy Veg•All® Tuna Casserole

 2 cups cooked medium egg noodles
 1 can (15 ounces) VEG•ALL® Original Mixed Vegetables,
     drained
 1 can (12 ounces) solid white tuna in water, drained
 1 can (10¾ ounces) cream of celery soup
1¼ cups whole milk
½ cup sour cream
 1 tablespoon chopped fresh dill
 1 cup crushed sour cream & onion potato chips

Combine all ingredients except potato chips in greased 1½-quart casserole dish.

Microwave, uncovered, on HIGH for 10 to 12 minutes or until very thick. Let cool for 10 minutes. Top with crushed potato chips before serving. *Makes 4 to 6 servings*

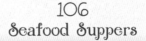

Shrimp Enchiladas

1 jar (1 pound 10 ounces) RAGÚ® Old World Style®
    Pasta Sauce
1 can (4 ounces) chopped green chilies, drained
1½ tablespoons chili powder
1 pound cooked shrimp, coarsely chopped
2 cups shredded Monterey Jack cheese (about 8 ounces)
1 container (8 ounces) sour cream
1 package (8 ounces) corn tortillas (12 tortillas), softened

1. Preheat oven to 400°F. In medium bowl, combine Ragú Pasta Sauce, chilies and chili powder. Evenly spread 1 cup sauce mixture in 13×9-inch baking dish; set aside.

2. In another medium bowl, combine shrimp, 1 cup cheese and sour cream. Evenly spread mixture onto tortillas; roll up. Arrange seam side down in prepared dish and top with remaining sauce mixture. Cover with aluminum foil and bake 20 minutes.

3. Remove foil and sprinkle with remaining 1 cup cheese. Bake an additional 5 minutes or until cheese is melted.   *Makes 6 servings*

Tip: To soften tortillas, arrange on a microwave-safe plate, cover with a dampened paper towel and microwave at HIGH 30 seconds.

Prep Time: 10 minutes • Cook Time: 40 minutes

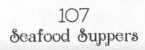

Salmon Casserole

 2 tablespoons butter
 2 cups sliced mushrooms
 1½ cups chopped carrots
 1 cup frozen peas
 1 cup chopped celery
 ½ cup chopped onion
 ½ cup chopped red bell pepper
 1 tablespoon chopped fresh parsley
 1 clove garlic, minced
 1 teaspoon salt
 ½ teaspoon black pepper
 ½ teaspoon dried basil
 4 cups cooked rice
 1 can (14 ounces) red salmon, drained and flaked
 1 can (10¾ ounces) condensed cream of mushroom soup,
    undiluted
 2 cups (8 ounces) grated Cheddar or American cheese
 ½ cup sliced black olives

1. Preheat oven to 350°F. Spray 2-quart casserole with nonstick cooking spray; set aside.

2. Melt butter in large skillet or Dutch oven over medium heat. Add mushrooms, carrots, peas, celery, onion, bell pepper, parsley, garlic, salt, black pepper and basil; cook and stir 10 minutes or until vegetables are tender. Add rice, salmon, soup and cheese; mix well.

3. Transfer to prepared casserole. Sprinkle olives over top. Bake 30 minutes or until hot and bubbly.   *Makes 8 servings*

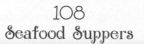

Seafood Lasagna

4 ounces lasagna noodles
1 jar (28 ounces) prepared pasta sauce or favorite
homemade sauce
1 package (6 ounces) frozen cooked salad shrimp, thawed
and drained
4 ounces surimi seafood, thawed and thinly sliced
½ cup low-fat ricotta cheese
¼ cup freshly grated Parmesan cheese
1 tablespoon minced fresh parsley
⅛ teaspoon black pepper
⅔ cup shredded low-fat mozzarella cheese

Heat oven to 375°F. Prepare lasagna noodles according to package directions. Pour pasta sauce into saucepan; simmer for 10 minutes until thickened and reduced to about 3 cups. Stir in shrimp and surimi seafood. Combine ricotta cheese, Parmesan cheese, parsley and pepper in small bowl.

To assemble lasagna, place half of noodles in 8×8-inch casserole. Top with half of seafood sauce; drop half of ricotta mixture by small teaspoonfuls over sauce. Sprinkle with half of mozzarella cheese. Repeat layers. Bake for 35 minutes or until bubbly. Let stand 10 minutes before cutting. *Makes 6 servings*

Favorite recipe from National Fisheries Institute

Starkist® Swiss Potato Pie

4 cups frozen shredded hash brown potatoes, thawed
2 cups shredded Swiss cheese
1 cup milk
4 large eggs, beaten
½ to 1 cup chopped green onions, including tops
½ cup chopped green bell pepper (optional)
½ cup sour cream
1 (3-ounce) STARKIST Flavor Fresh Pouch® Tuna (Albacore)
½ teaspoon garlic powder

In large bowl, combine all ingredients. Pour into lightly greased deep 10-inch pie plate. Bake in 350°F oven 1 hour and 20 minutes or until golden and crusty. Let stand a few minutes before slicing into serving portions.   *Makes 6 servings*

Egg Noodle-Crab Casserole

12 ounces wide egg noodles, uncooked
1 can (10¾ ounces) Cheddar cheese soup
1 cup milk
1 tablespoon dried onions
¼ teaspoon paprika
¼ teaspoon dried marjoram
1 pound crabmeat
1 cup SONOMA® Dried Tomato Halves, snipped into strips, parboiled and drained

Cook noodles according to package directions until al dente. Set aside and keep warm.

In medium bowl, combine soup and milk. Stir in onions, paprika and marjoram. Place noodles in 2½- to 3-quart casserole. Break up crabmeat into bite-size pieces; sprinkle crabmeat and tomatoes over noodles. Pour soup mixture over crab mixture; mix well.

Cover and bake in 350°F oven for 30 minutes or until hot and bubbly.
Makes 6 servings

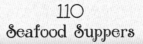

Spicy Snapper & Black Beans

1½ pounds fresh red snapper fillets, cut into 4 portions (6 ounces each)
Juice of 1 lime
½ teaspoon coarsely ground black pepper
Nonstick cooking spray
1 cup GUILTLESS GOURMET® Spicy Black Bean Dip
½ cup water
½ cup (about 35) crushed GUILTLESS GOURMET® Baked Tortilla Chips (yellow or white corn)
1 cup GUILTLESS GOURMET® Roasted Red Pepper Salsa

Wash fish thoroughly; pat dry with paper towels. Place fish in 13×9-inch glass baking dish. Pour lime juice over top; sprinkle with pepper. Cover and refrigerate 1 hour.

Preheat oven to 350°F. Coat 11×7-inch glass baking dish with cooking spray. Combine bean dip and water in small bowl; spread 1 cup bean mixture in bottom of prepared baking dish. Place fish over bean mixture, discarding juice. Spread remaining bean mixture over top of fish; sprinkle with crushed chips.

Bake about 20 minutes or until chips are lightly browned and fish turns opaque and flakes easily when tested with fork. To serve, divide fish among 4 serving plates; spoon ¼ cup salsa over top of each serving. *Makes 4 servings*

Note: This recipe can be made with 4 boneless skinless chicken breast halves in place of red snapper fillets. Prepare as directed and bake about 40 minutes or until chicken is no longer pink in center. Serve as directed.

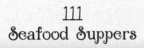

Broccoli-Stuffed Shells

1 tablespoon butter or margarine
¼ cup chopped onion
1 cup ricotta cheese
1 egg
2 cups chopped cooked broccoli *or* 1 package
    (10 ounces) frozen chopped broccoli,
    thawed and well drained
1 cup (4 ounces) shredded Monterey Jack cheese
20 jumbo pasta shells
1 can (28 ounces) crushed tomatoes in purée
1 packet (1 ounce) HIDDEN VALLEY® The Original
    Ranch® Salad Dressing & Seasoning Mix
¼ cup grated Parmesan cheese

Preheat oven to 350°F. In small skillet, melt butter over medium heat. Add onion; cook until onion is tender but not browned. Remove from heat; cool. In large bowl, stir ricotta cheese and egg until well blended. Add broccoli and Monterey Jack cheese; mix well. In large pot of boiling water, cook pasta shells 8 to 10 minutes or just until tender; drain. Rinse under cold running water; drain again. Stuff each shell with about 2 tablespoons broccoli-cheese mixture.

In medium bowl, combine tomatoes, sautéed onion and salad dressing & seasoning mix; mix well. Pour one third of the tomato mixture into 13×9-inch baking dish. Arrange filled shells in dish. Spoon remaining tomato mixture over top. Sprinkle with Parmesan cheese. Bake, covered, until hot and bubbly, about 30 minutes. *Makes 4 servings*

Pesto Lasagna

  1 package (16 ounces) uncooked lasagna noodles
  3 tablespoons olive oil
1½ cups chopped onions
  3 cloves garlic, finely chopped
  2 packages (10 ounces each) frozen chopped spinach,
     thawed and squeezed dry
    Salt
    Black pepper
  2 cups (16 ounces) ricotta cheese
  1 cup prepared pesto sauce
  ½ cup grated Parmesan cheese
  ½ cup pine nuts, toasted
  3 cups (12 ounces) shredded mozzarella cheese
    Strips of roasted red pepper (optional)

1. Preheat oven to 350°F. Spray 13×9-inch pan with nonstick cooking spray. Partially cook lasagna noodles according to package directions.

2. Heat oil in large skillet over medium-high heat. Cook and stir onions and garlic until transparent. Add spinach; cook and stir about 5 minutes. Season with salt and pepper. Transfer to large bowl.

3. Add ricotta cheese, pesto, Parmesan cheese and pine nuts to spinach mixture; mix well.

4. Layer 5 lasagna noodles, slightly overlapping, in prepared pan. Top with one third of ricotta mixture and one third of mozzarella. Repeat layers twice.

5. Bake about 35 minutes or until hot and bubbly. Garnish with red bell pepper. *Makes 8 servings*

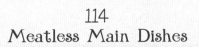

Baked Ziti with Walnuts

1 cup uncooked ziti pasta
1 box (10 ounces) BIRDS EYE® frozen Peas & Pearl Onions
1 cup tomato sauce
½ cup chopped walnuts
1 tablespoon olive oil
2 tablespoons grated Parmesan cheese

• Preheat oven to 350°F.

• Cook ziti according to package directions; drain and set aside.

• In large bowl, combine vegetables, tomato sauce, walnuts and oil. Add ziti; toss well.

• Place mixture in 13×9-inch baking pan. Sprinkle with cheese.

• Bake 20 minutes or until heated through.   *Makes 4 servings*

Prep Time: 10 minutes • Cook Time: 20 minutes

Italian Vegetable Strata

1 loaf (12 ounces) Italian bread, cut into 1-inch slices
3 cups RAGÚ® Chunky Pasta Sauce
1½ cups shredded mozzarella cheese (about 6 ounces)
6 eggs, beaten
1 cup water
1 jar (7 ounces) roasted red peppers packed in oil, drained
1 medium zucchini, thinly sliced
¼ cup grated Parmesan cheese

Preheat oven to 350°F. In greased 13×9-inch baking dish, arrange bread slices; set aside.

In large bowl, combine remaining ingredients; pour mixture over bread. Let stand 15 minutes. Bake covered 35 minutes or until vegetables are tender.   *Makes 6 servings*

Eggplant Parmesan

½ cup olive or vegetable oil
1 medium eggplant (about 1½ pounds), peeled, sliced
1 carton (15 ounces) ricotta cheese
1 can (15 ounces) CONTADINA® Italian-Style Tomato Sauce
1 clove garlic, minced
½ teaspoon dried oregano leaves, crushed
½ cup CONTADINA Seasoned Bread Crumbs
2 tablespoons grated Parmesan cheese

1. Heat oil in large skillet. Add eggplant; cook for 2 to 3 minutes on each side or until tender. Remove from oil with slotted spoon. Drain on paper towels.

2. Place half of eggplant slices in greased 12×7½-inch baking dish. Spoon half of ricotta cheese over eggplant.

3. Combine tomato sauce, garlic and oregano in small bowl. Pour half of tomato sauce mixture over ricotta cheese.

4. Combine bread crumbs and Parmesan cheese in separate small bowl; sprinkle half over top of sauce mixture. Repeat layers.

5. Bake in preheated 350°F oven for 30 minutes or until sauce is bubbly.   *Makes 6 servings*

Prep Time: 20 minutes • Cook Time: 30 minutes

Chili Relleno Casserole

1½ cups (6 ounces) SARGENTO® Light 4 Cheese Mexican
    Shredded Cheese or SARGENTO® Light Shredded
    Cheese for Tacos, divided
1 can (12 ounces) evaporated skim milk
¾ cup (6 ounces) fat-free liquid egg substitute *or* 3 eggs,
    beaten
6 (7-inch) corn tortillas, torn into 2-inch pieces
2 cans (4 ounces each) chopped green chilies
½ cup mild chunky salsa
¼ teaspoon salt (optional)
2 tablespoons chopped fresh cilantro
    Light or fat-free sour cream (optional)

1. Coat 10-inch deep-dish pie plate or 8-inch square baking dish with nonstick cooking spray. In medium bowl, combine 1 cup cheese, milk, egg substitute, tortillas, chilies, salsa and salt, if desired. Mix well; pour into prepared dish.

2. Bake at 375°F 30 to 32 minutes or until set. Remove from oven; sprinkle with remaining ½ cup cheese and cilantro. Return to oven; bake 1 minute or until cheese is melted. Serve with sour cream, if desired. *Makes 4 servings*

Chili relleno literally means "stuffed
pepper." Traditionally the mild green
peppers are stuffed with cheese, coated
with batter and deep fried. This casserole
version provides some of the classic
Mexican flavors in a lighter dish.

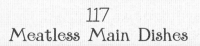

Vegetable Lasagna

1 container (15 ounces) ricotta cheese
1 egg
1 teaspoon Italian seasoning
1 tablespoon olive oil
2 zucchini or yellow squash, thinly sliced
1 red bell pepper, chopped
1 package (10 ounces) frozen chopped spinach, thawed and
    squeezed dry
2 cups *French's*® French Fried Onions, divided
3 cups (28-ounce jar) prepared Alfredo sauce
    (or two 16-ounce jars)
9 pieces oven-ready lasagna noodles
2 cups (8 ounces) shredded mozzarella cheese, divided
¼ cup grated Parmesan cheese

1. Preheat oven to 375°F. Combine ricotta cheese, egg and Italian seasoning in medium bowl; set aside.

2. Heat oil in 12-inch nonstick skillet over medium-high heat. Add squash and bell pepper; sauté 5 minutes or until crisp-tender. Stir in spinach and *1 cup* French Fried Onions; set aside.

3. To assemble lasagna, spoon 1 cup Alfredo sauce into greased 13×9-inch baking dish. Place 3 uncooked noodles crosswise over sauce. Evenly spread pasta with half of ricotta mixture. Top with half of vegetable mixture, ½ cup mozzarella cheese and ½ cup sauce. Repeat layers once.

4. Arrange remaining noodles on top and cover with remaining 1 cup sauce and 1 cup mozzarella cheese. Bake, covered, 30 minutes or until noodles are tender. Sprinkle with remaining *1 cup* onions and Parmesan cheese. Uncover and bake 5 minutes or until onions are golden. *Makes 6 to 8 servings*

Prep Time: 15 minutes • Cook Time: 40 minutes

Italian Three-Cheese Macaroni

Nonstick cooking spray
2 cups uncooked elbow macaroni
4 tablespoons butter
3 tablespoons all-purpose flour
1 teaspoon Italian seasoning
½ to 1 teaspoon black pepper
½ teaspoon salt
2 cups milk
¾ cup (3 ounces) shredded Cheddar cheese
¼ cup grated Parmesan cheese
1 can (14½ ounces) diced tomatoes, drained
1 cup (4 ounces) shredded mozzarella cheese
½ cup dry bread crumbs

1. Preheat oven to 350°F. Spray 2-quart round casserole with nonstick cooking spray.

2. Cook macaroni according to package directions until al dente. Drain and set aside.

3. Meanwhile, melt butter in medium saucepan over medium heat. Add flour, Italian seasoning, pepper and salt, stirring until smooth. Gradually add milk, stirring constantly until slightly thickened. Add Cheddar and Parmesan; stir until cheeses melt.

4. Layer half of pasta, half of tomatoes and half of cheese sauce in prepared dish. Repeat layers.

5. Combine mozzarella and bread crumbs in small bowl. Sprinkle evenly over casserole. Spray bread crumb mixture several times with cooking spray.

6. Bake, covered, about 30 minutes or until hot and bubbly. Uncover and bake 5 minutes or until top is golden brown.   *Makes 4 servings*

Baked Bow-Tie Pasta in Mushroom Cream Sauce

1 teaspoon olive oil
1 large onion, thinly sliced
1 package (10 ounces) sliced mushrooms
⅛ teaspoon ground black pepper
1 jar (1 pound) RAGÚ® Cheesy!® Light Parmesan Alfredo Sauce
8 ounces bow tie pasta, cooked and drained
1 tablespoon grated Parmesan cheese
1 tablespoon plain dry bread crumbs (optional)

1. Preheat oven to 400°F. In 10-inch nonstick skillet, heat olive oil over medium heat and cook onion, mushrooms and pepper, stirring frequently, 10 minutes or until vegetables are golden. Stir in Ragú Alfredo Sauce.

2. In 2-quart shallow baking dish, combine sauce mixture with hot pasta. Sprinkle with cheese combined with bread crumbs. Cover with aluminum foil and bake 20 minutes. Remove foil and bake an additional 5 minutes.   *Makes 6 servings*

Prep Time: 10 minutes • Cook Time: 35 minutes

Chilaquiles

2 tablespoons vegetable oil
1 medium onion, chopped
1 package (1.0 ounce) LAWRY'S® Taco Spices & Seasonings
1 can (28 ounces) diced tomatoes in juice
1 can (4 ounces) diced green chiles (optional)
6 ounces plain tortilla chips
4 cups shredded Monterey Jack cheese (about 16 ounces)
1 cup (8 ounces) sour cream
½ cup shredded cheddar cheese (about 2 ounces)

In large skillet, heat oil over medium high heat. Add onion and cook until tender. Add Taco Spices & Seasonings, tomatoes and chiles; mix well. Bring to a boil; reduce heat to low and cook, uncovered, 10 minutes, stirring occasionally. Spray 2-quart casserole dish with nonstick cooking spray; arrange ½ of tortilla chips, sauce and Monterey Jack cheese. Repeat layers; top with sour cream. Bake in 350°F oven for 25 minutes. Sprinkle with cheddar cheese and bake 5 minutes longer. Let stand 10 minutes before serving.

Makes 6 servings

Meal Idea: Serve with a marinated vegetable salad and fresh fruit.

Prep Time: 15 minutes • Cook Time: 45 minutes

Mom's Baked Mostaccioli

  1 container (16 ounces) ricotta cheese
  2 eggs
¼ cup grated Parmesan cheese
    Garlic powder
    Black pepper
    Italian seasoning
  1 package (16 ounces) mostaccioli, cooked and drained
  1 jar (26 ounces) prepared pasta sauce
1½ cups (6 ounces) shredded mozzarella cheese

1. Preheat oven to 350°F. Spray 13×9-inch casserole with nonstick cooking spray.

2. Combine ricotta cheese, eggs and Parmesan cheese in medium bowl. Season with garlic powder, pepper and Italian seasoning; mix well.

3. Place half of pasta in prepared casserole. Spread ricotta mixture evenly over pasta. Spoon remaining pasta over ricotta mixture. Top with pasta sauce and mozzarella cheese.

4. Bake 30 minutes or until hot and bubbly.

Makes 8 servings

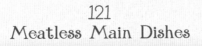

121

Broccoli & Cheddar Noodle Casserole

1 package (12 ounces) dry wide egg noodles
3 tablespoons margarine or butter, divided
2 cups chopped onions
4 cups broccoli flowerets
1 can (14.5 ounces) CONTADINA® Stewed Tomatoes, undrained
1 can (6 ounces) CONTADINA Tomato Paste
1 package (1½ ounces) spaghetti sauce seasoning mix
2 cups water
1 teaspoon garlic salt
1½ cups (6 ounces) shredded Cheddar cheese
½ cup CONTADINA Seasoned Italian Bread Crumbs

1. Cook noodles according to package directions; drain.

2. Meanwhile, melt 2 tablespoons margarine in 5-quart saucepan; sauté onions until tender.

3. Stir in broccoli, undrained tomatoes, tomato paste, seasoning mix, water and garlic salt. Bring to a boil. Reduce heat; simmer, uncovered, for 10 minutes, stirring occasionally. Stir in cooked noodles.

4. Layer half of noodle mixture in 13×9×2-inch baking dish. Sprinkle with cheese. Layer with remaining noodle mixture.

5. Melt remaining 1 tablespoon margarine; stir in crumbs. Sprinkle over casserole; cover and bake in preheated 350°F oven 20 minutes. Uncover; bake 5 minutes.

Makes 6 servings

Prep Time: 25 minutes • Cook Time: 25 minutes

Cheese Enchiladas with Green Chiles

1 can (10 ounces) ORTEGA® Enchilada Sauce
1 cup ORTEGA Salsa-Homestyle Recipe
15 (6-inch) corn tortillas
1 pound Monterey Jack cheese, sliced into 15 strips
1 can (7 ounces) ORTEGA Whole Green Chiles, sliced into
    3 strips each, 15 strips total
1 cup (4 ounces) shredded Monterey Jack cheese

PREHEAT oven to 350°F.

COMBINE enchilada sauce and salsa in medium bowl; mix well. Pour
1½ cups sauce mixture onto bottom of ungreased 13×9-inch baking pan.

HEAT tortillas, one at a time, in lightly greased medium skillet over
medium heat for 20 seconds on each side or until soft. Place 1 strip
cheese and 1 strip chile in center of each tortilla; roll up. Place seam-side
down in baking pan. Repeat with remaining tortillas, cheese and chiles.
Ladle *remaining* sauce mixture over enchiladas; sprinkle with shredded
cheese.

BAKE, covered, for 20 minutes. Remove cover; bake for additional
5 minutes or until heated through and cheese is melted.

Makes 6 to 8 servings

Monterey Jack is named for the town of
Monterey, California where the cheese
originated. It is a mild-flavored semisoft
cheese, high in moisture and good for
melting, which makes it a popular choice
for sandwiches as well as casseroles.

Double Spinach Bake

8 ounces uncooked spinach fettuccine noodles
1 cup sliced mushrooms
1 green onion, finely chopped
1 clove garlic, minced
4 to 5 cups fresh spinach, coarsely chopped *or* 1 package
    (10 ounces) frozen spinach, thawed and drained
1 tablespoon water
1 container (15 ounces) ricotta cheese
¼ cup milk
1 egg
½ teaspoon ground nutmeg
½ teaspoon black pepper
½ cup (2 ounces) shredded Swiss cheese

1. Preheat oven to 350°F. Cook noodles according to package directions. Drain and set aside.

2. Spray medium skillet with nonstick cooking spray. Add mushrooms, green onion and garlic; cook and stir over medium heat until mushrooms are softened. Add spinach and water; cover and cook about 3 minutes or until spinach is wilted.

3. Combine ricotta cheese, milk, egg, nutmeg and black pepper in large bowl. Gently stir in noodles and vegetables; toss to coat evenly.

4. Lightly coat shallow 1½-quart casserole with nonstick cooking spray. Spread noodle mixture in casserole. Sprinkle with Swiss cheese.

5. Bake 25 to 30 minutes or until knife inserted halfway into center comes out clean. *Makes 6 servings*

Viking Vegetable Cassoulet

4 cups sliced mushrooms
2 tablespoons Lucini Premium Select extra virgin olive oil
2 large onions, thickly sliced
1 large clove garlic, minced
2 medium zucchini, cut into 1-inch pieces
1½ cups sliced yellow squash
2 cans (16 ounces each) white beans, drained
1 can (14½ ounces) plum tomatoes, cut up, with juice
⅓ cup chopped parsley
1 teaspoon dried basil, crushed
½ teaspoon dried oregano, crushed
½ cup bread crumbs
1 teaspoon butter, melted
2 cups (8 ounces) shredded JARLSBERG Cheese

In large deep skillet, brown mushrooms in oil. Add onions and garlic; sauté 5 minutes. Add zucchini and yellow squash; sauté until vegetables are crisp-tender. Stir in beans, tomatoes, parsley, basil and oregano.

Spoon into 2-quart baking dish. Combine bread crumbs and butter in small bowl. Sprinkle bread crumbs around edge of dish. Bake at 350°F 20 minutes. Top with cheese and bake 20 minutes more.

Makes 6 to 8 servings

Chilies Rellenos Bake

  3 eggs, separated
¾ cup milk
¾ cup all-purpose flour
½ teaspoon salt
  1 tablespoon butter or margarine
½ cup chopped onion
  2 cans (7 ounces each) whole green chilies, drained
  8 slices (1 ounce each) Monterey Jack cheese, cut into halves
    Toppings: sour cream, sliced green onions, pitted ripe olive
      slices, guacamole and salsa

1. Preheat oven to 350°F. Grease 13×9-inch baking dish.

2. Combine egg yolks, milk, flour and salt in blender or food processor container. Cover and blend until smooth. Pour into bowl; let stand until ready to use.

3. Melt butter in small skillet over medium heat. Add onion; cook and stir until tender.

4. Pat chilies dry with paper towels. Slit each chili lengthwise and carefully remove seeds. Place 2 halves of cheese and 1 tablespoon onion in each chili; reshape chilies to cover cheese. Place in single layer in prepared baking dish.

5. Beat egg whites in small clean bowl until soft peaks form; fold into egg yolk mixture. Pour over chilies in baking dish.

6. Bake 20 to 25 minutes or until casserole is puffed and knife inserted in center comes out clean. Broil 4 inches below heat 30 seconds or until top is golden brown. Serve with desired toppings.

Makes 4 servings

Lentil-Rice Casserole

2⅔ cups vegetable or chicken broth
¾ cup uncooked lentils
¾ cup chopped onion
½ cup uncooked brown rice
½ cup (2 ounces) shredded Swiss cheese
½ cup dry white wine
2 cloves garlic, mashed or ¼ teaspoon garlic powder
½ teaspoon dried basil leaves
½ teaspoon dried oregano leaves
½ teaspoon dried thyme leaves
⅛ teaspoon pepper
¾ cup SONOMA® Dried Tomato Halves, snipped into strips
8 thin slices Swiss cheese

Combine all ingredients except dried tomatoes and cheese slices. Pour into ungreased 1½- to 2-quart casserole. Bake, uncovered, at 350°F for 1½ to 2 hours or until rice and lentils are tender. Stir twice during baking. Stir in tomato strips; top casserole with sliced cheese and bake 2 to 3 minutes more. *Makes 4 servings*

Southwestern Tortilla Stack

1 (30-ounce) can vegetarian refried beans
½ cup sour cream
1 (4-ounce) can chopped green chilies, drained
½ teaspoon ground cumin
3 (10-inch) flour tortillas
1 cup (4 ounces) shredded Cheddar cheese

Preheat oven to 425°F. Grease 10-inch round casserole. Combine beans, sour cream, chilies and cumin. Place one tortilla in bottom of prepared casserole. Top with half of bean mixture and one third of cheese. Top with second tortilla; repeat layers of beans and cheese. Cover with remaining tortilla; sprinkle with remaining cheese.

Cover and bake 20 minutes or until heated through. Cut into wedges. Serve with salsa, if desired. *Makes 4 to 6 servings*

Greek-Style Stuffed Shells

**1 jar (1 pound 10 ounces) RAGÚ® Chunky Gardenstyle Pasta
   Sauce**
1 container (15 ounces) ricotta cheese
8 ounces feta cheese, crumbled
1 large egg, lightly beaten
1 teaspoon dried oregano leaves, crushed
6 ounces jumbo shells pasta, cooked and drained (about 21)

1. Preheat oven to 350°F. In 13×9-inch baking dish, evenly spread
1 cup Ragú Pasta Sauce; set aside.

2. In large bowl, combine cheeses, egg and oregano. Fill shells with
cheese mixture, then arrange in baking dish. Evenly top with
remaining sauce.

3. Bake 30 minutes or until sauce is bubbling. Garnish, if desired,
with sliced pitted ripe olives.   *Makes 6 servings*

Tip: Try using a small ice cream scoop to neatly fill shells.

Prep Time: 20 minutes • Cook Time: 30 minutes

Monterey Spaghetti Casserole

4 ounces uncooked spaghetti
1 cup sour cream
1 egg, beaten
2 cups (8 ounces) shredded Monterey Jack cheese
¼ cup grated Parmesan cheese
**1 package (10 ounces) frozen chopped spinach, thawed and
   drained**
1⅓ cups *French's*® French Fried Onions, divided

Preheat oven to 350°F. Cook spaghetti according to package directions
using shortest cooking time. Drain.

Combine sour cream and egg in 8-inch square baking dish. Stir in
spaghetti, cheeses, spinach and *⅔ cup* French Fried Onions.

Cover; bake 30 minutes or until heated through. Stir. Top with remaining ⅔ *cup* onions. Bake, uncovered, 5 minutes or until onions are golden. *Makes 4 servings*

Prep Time: 10 minutes • Cook Time: 35 minutes

Vegetarian Orzo & Feta Bake

1 package (16 ounces) orzo pasta
1 can (4¼ ounces) chopped black olives, drained
2 cloves garlic, minced
1 sheet (24×18 inches) heavy-duty foil, lightly sprayed with nonstick cooking spray
1 can (about 14 ounces) diced Italian-style tomatoes, undrained
1 can (14 ounces) vegetable broth
2 tablespoons olive oil
6 to 8 ounces feta cheese, cut into ½-inch cubes

1. Preheat oven to 450°F.

2. Combine orzo, olives and garlic in medium bowl. Place orzo mixture in center of foil sheet.

3. Fold sides of foil up around orzo mixture, but do not seal.

4. In same bowl, combine tomatoes with juices, broth and oil. Pour over orzo mixture. Top with cheese.

5. Double fold sides and ends of foil to seal packet, leaving head space for heat circulation. Place packet on baking sheet.

6. Bake 22 to 24 minutes or until pasta is tender. Remove from oven. Let stand 5 minutes. Open packet and transfer contents to serving plates. *Makes 6 servings*

Tomato-Bread Casserole

3 tablespoons butter or margarine, softened
½ pound loaf French bread, sliced
1½ pounds tomatoes, thinly sliced
1 cup lowfat cottage or ricotta cheese
1 can (14½ ounces) diced tomatoes, drained (reserving liquid)
¾ teaspoon LAWRY'S® Seasoned Salt
½ teaspoon oregano
¼ cup olive oil
¾ teaspoon LAWRY'S® Garlic Powder With Parsley
½ cup shredded Parmesan cheese
¼ cup chopped parsley (garnish)

Spread bread slices with butter; cut into large cubes. Arrange on baking sheet. Toast in 350°F oven until golden. Place ½ of cubes in greased 13×9×2-inch baking dish. Top bread cubes with ½ of fresh tomato slices, ½ of cottage cheese, ½ of canned tomatoes, ½ reserved tomato liquid, ½ of Seasoned Salt, ½ of oregano, ½ of oil and ½ of Garlic Powder With Parsley. Layer again. Sprinkle with Parmesan cheese. Cover and bake in 350°F oven for 40 minutes. Uncover and bake 5 minutes longer to brown top. Garnish with parsley.

Makes 6 to 8 servings

Meal Idea: Serve with marinated mushrooms.

Prep Time: 15 minutes • Cook Time: 45 minutes

Red, White and Black Bean Casserole

2 tablespoons olive oil
1 yellow or green bell pepper, cut into ½-inch strips
½ cup sliced green onions
1 can (14½ ounces) chunky-style salsa
1 can (4½ ounces) green chilies, drained
1 package (1½ ounces) taco seasoning mix
2 tablespoons chopped fresh cilantro
½ teaspoon salt
2 cups cooked white rice
1 can (19 ounces) white cannellini beans, rinsed and drained
1 can (15½ ounces) red kidney beans, rinsed and drained
1 can (15½ ounces) black beans, rinsed and drained
1 cup (4 ounces) shredded Cheddar cheese, divided
1 package (6-inch) flour tortillas

HEAT oil in large saucepan over medium-high heat. Cook and stir pepper and green onions about 5 minutes. Add salsa, chilies, taco seasoning, cilantro and salt; cook 5 minutes, stirring occasionally. Stir in rice and beans. Remove from heat; stir in ½ cup cheese.

SPOON mixture into prepared baking dish. Sprinkle remaining ½ cup cheese evenly over top. Cover and bake 30 to 40 minutes or until heated through. Serve with warm tortillas.

Makes 6 servings

Mexican-Style Stuffed Peppers

      8 medium green bell peppers, halved and seeded
      3 cups cooked long-grain white rice
      1 package (10 ounces) frozen peas and carrots
      1 cup whole kernel corn
     ½ cup chopped green onions
    1¾ cups ORTEGA® Salsa-Homestyle Recipe, divided
    1½ cups 4-cheese Mexican blend, divided

PREHEAT oven to 375°F.

PLACE bell peppers in microwave-safe dish with 3 tablespoons water. Cover with plastic wrap. Microwave on HIGH (100%) power for 4 to 5 minutes or until slightly tender. Drain.

COMBINE rice, peas and carrots, corn, green onions, ¾ cup salsa and 1 cup cheese in large bowl. Fill each pepper with about ½ cup rice mixture. Place peppers in ungreased 13×9×2-inch baking dish; top with remaining salsa and cheese.

BAKE uncovered for 20 to 25 minutes. Uncover; bake for additional 5 minutes or until heated through and cheese is melted.

Makes 8 servings

Harvest Casserole

      2 cups USA lentils, rinsed and cooked
      2 cups chopped fresh or frozen broccoli
    1½ cups cooked rice
    1½ cups (6 ounces) shredded Cheddar cheese
      1 tablespoon soy sauce
     ½ teaspoon salt (optional)
     ¼ teaspoon dried thyme
     ¼ teaspoon dried marjoram
     ¼ teaspoon dried rosemary
      4 eggs
      1 cup milk

Preheat oven to 350°F.

Mix lentils, broccoli, rice, cheese, soy sauce, salt, thyme, marjoram and rosemary in large bowl. Place mixture in greased 9-inch casserole dish.

Beat eggs and milk in medium bowl. Pour egg mixture over lentil mixture. Bake 45 minutes or until lightly browned. Top with additional shredded Cheddar cheese, if desired.   *Makes 8 servings*

Favorite recipe from USA Dry Pea & Lentil Council

Pasta with Four Cheeses

- ¾ **cup uncooked ziti or rigatoni**
- 3 **tablespoons butter, divided**
- ½ **cup grated CUCINA CLASSICA ITALIANA® Parmesan cheese, divided**
- ¼ **teaspoon ground nutmeg, divided**
- ¼ **cup GALBANI® Mascarpone**
- ¾ **cup (about 3½ ounces) shredded mozzarella cheese**
- ¾ **cup (about 3½ ounces) shredded BEL PAESE® semi-soft cheese**

Preheat oven to 350°F. Lightly grease 1-quart casserole. Set aside.

In large saucepan of boiling water, cook pasta until tender but still firm. Drain in colander. Place in large mixing bowl. Stir in 1½ tablespoons butter, ¼ cup Parmesan cheese and ⅛ teaspoon nutmeg.

Spread one fourth of pasta mixture into prepared casserole. Spoon Mascarpone onto pasta. Layer with one fourth of pasta. Top with mozzarella. Add third layer of pasta. Sprinkle with Bel Paese® cheese. Top with remaining pasta. Dot with remaining 1½ tablespoons butter. Sprinkle with remaining ¼ cup Parmesan cheese and ⅛ teaspoon nutmeg. Bake until golden brown, about 20 minutes.

Makes 4 servings

Double Cheese Strata

10 to 12 slices Italian bread, about ½ inch thick
⅔ cup (about 5 ounces) sharp Cheddar light cold pack cheese food, softened
1⅓ cups *French's*® French Fried Onions
1 package (10 ounces) frozen chopped broccoli, thawed and drained
½ cup (2 ounces) shredded Swiss cheese
3 cups milk
5 eggs
2 tablespoons *French's*® Bold n' Spicy Brown Mustard
½ teaspoon salt
¼ teaspoon ground white pepper

Grease 3-quart baking dish. Spread bread slices with Cheddar cheese. Arrange slices in single layer in bottom of prepared baking dish, pressing to fit. Layer French Fried Onions, broccoli and Swiss cheese over bread.

Beat together milk, eggs, mustard, salt and pepper in medium bowl until well blended. Pour egg mixture over layers. Let stand 10 minutes. Preheat oven to 350°F. Bake 35 minutes or until knife inserted in center comes out clean. (Cover loosely with foil near end of baking if top becomes too brown.) Cool on wire rack 10 minutes. Cut into squares to serve. *Makes 8 servings*

Prep Time: 15 minutes • Cook Time: 35 minutes

Greek Spinach and Feta Pie

⅓ **cup butter, melted**
2 **eggs**
1 **package (10 ounces) frozen chopped spinach, thawed and**
    squeezed dry
1 **container (15 ounces) ricotta cheese**
1 **package (4 ounces) crumbled feta cheese**
¾ **teaspoon finely grated lemon peel**
¼ **teaspoon black pepper**
⅛ **teaspoon ground nutmeg**
1 **package (16 ounces) frozen phyllo dough, thawed**

Preheat oven to 350°F. Brush 13×9-inch baking dish lightly with butter.

Beat eggs in medium bowl. Stir in spinach, ricotta, feta, lemon peel, pepper and nutmeg. Set aside.

Unwrap phyllo dough; remove 8 sheets. Cut dough in half crosswise forming 16 rectangles about 13×8½ inches. Cover dough with damp cloth or plastic wrap to keep moist while assembling pie. Reserve remaining dough for another use.

Place 1 piece of dough in prepared dish; brush top lightly with butter. Top with another piece of dough and brush lightly with butter. Continue layering with 6 pieces of dough, brushing each lightly with butter. Spoon spinach mixture evenly over dough.

Top spinach mixture with piece of dough; brush lightly with butter. Repeat layering with remaining 7 pieces of dough, brushing each piece lightly with butter.

Bake, uncovered, 35 to 40 minutes or until golden brown.

Makes 6 servings

Serving Suggestion: Serve with a Greek salad of cucumbers, tomatoes and red onions on a bed of romaine lettuce and drizzled with red wine vinegar salad dressing.

Lasagna Florentine

2 tablespoons olive oil
3 medium carrots, finely chopped
1 package (8 to 10 ounces) sliced mushrooms
1 medium onion, finely chopped
2 cloves garlic, finely chopped
1 jar (1 pound 10 ounces) RAGÚ® Robusto®! Pasta Sauce
1 container (15 ounces) ricotta cheese
2 cups (8 ounces) shredded mozzarella cheese, divided
1 box (10 ounces) frozen chopped spinach, thawed and
    squeezed dry
2 eggs
¼ cup grated Parmesan cheese
1 teaspoon salt
1 teaspoon dried Italian seasoning
16 lasagna noodles, cooked and drained

Preheat oven to 375°F. In 12-inch skillet, heat olive oil over medium
heat. Cook carrots, mushrooms, onion and garlic in oil until carrots
are almost tender, about 5 minutes. Stir in Ragú Pasta Sauce; heat
through.

Meanwhile, in medium bowl, combine ricotta cheese, 1½ cups
mozzarella cheese, spinach, eggs, Parmesan cheese, salt and Italian
seasoning; set aside.

In 13×9-inch baking dish, evenly spread ½ cup sauce mixture. Arrange
4 lasagna noodles lengthwise over sauce, overlapping edges slightly.
Spread ⅓ of ricotta mixture over noodles; repeat layers, ending with
noodles. Top with remaining sauce and ½ cup mozzarella cheese.
Cover with foil and bake 40 minutes. Remove foil and continue baking
10 minutes or until bubbling.   *Makes 8 servings*

Eggplant Pasta Bake

4 ounces dry bow-tie pasta
1 pound eggplant, diced
1 clove garlic, minced
¼ cup olive oil
1½ cups shredded Monterey Jack cheese, divided
1 cup sliced green onions
½ cup grated Parmesan cheese
**1 can (14½ ounces) DEL MONTE® Diced Tomatoes with
   Basil, Garlic & Oregano, undrained**

1. Preheat oven to 350°F. Cook pasta according to package directions; drain.

2. Cook eggplant and garlic in oil in large skillet over medium-high heat until tender.

3. Toss eggplant with cooked pasta, 1 cup Monterey Jack cheese, green onions and Parmesan cheese.

4. Place in greased 9-inch square baking dish. Top with undrained tomatoes and remaining ½ cup Monterey Jack cheese. Bake 15 minutes or until heated through.   *Makes 6 servings*

Prep and Cook Time: 30 minutes

When purchasing eggplant, look for
a firm eggplant that is heavy for its size,
with tight, glossy, deeply-colored skin.
The stem should be bright green.
Dull skin and rust-colored spots
are signs of old age.

Vegetable Gratin

2 tablespoons olive oil
3 small *or* 1 large zucchini, sliced into ¼-inch slices
⅛ teaspoon *each* salt, thyme, rosemary and freshly
    ground black pepper, divided
1 (6.5-ounce) package ALOUETTE® Savory Vegetable
2 cups fresh broccoli florets
2 small yellow squash, sliced
1 small onion, sliced
1 cup crushed BRETON® Wheat Crackers

• Preheat oven to 350°F. Place oil in medium-sized gratin or shallow baking dish.

• Layer zucchini in prepared dish. Sprinkle zucchini lightly with half each of salt, thyme, rosemary and pepper.

• Place 3 tablespoons Alouette on top of zucchini.

• Layer with broccoli, yellow squash, onion, remaining seasonings and Alouette until dish is filled.

• Sprinkle with cracker crumbs; cover with foil and bake 20 minutes.

• Remove foil and bake another 20 minutes. Brown lightly under broiler 1 to 2 minutes. Serve hot or at room temperature.

Makes 6 to 8 servings

Note: Vegetable Gratin is great served with grilled chicken or steak.

Fruit and Spicy
Sausage Stuffing

¼ cup dried cranberries, chopped
¼ cup dried apricots, chopped
1 tangerine, peeled, sectioned, seeded and diced
   Grated zest of 1 tangerine
   Juice of 3 tangerines
1 pound HILLSHIRE FARM® Smoked Sausage, casing
   removed and chopped
1 onion, diced
2 ribs celery, chopped
¼ cup diced peeled pear
6 to 8 cups bread crumbs
1 tablespoon chopped fresh tarragon *or* 1 teaspoon dried
   tarragon leaves
   Salt and black pepper to taste
1 cup vegetable or chicken broth, heated

Preheat oven to 400°F.

Combine cranberries, apricots, diced tangerine, tangerine zest and
tangerine juice in small bowl; set aside to plump dried fruit. Sauté
Smoked Sausage, onion, celery and pear in small skillet over
medium-high heat until pear is barely tender.

Toss sausage mixture with cranberry mixture, bread crumbs, tarragon,
salt and pepper in large bowl; add hot broth to moisten. Turn mixture
into greased casserole or baking pan; bake, uncovered, 45 minutes or
until browned on top.   *Makes 6 to 8 servings*

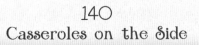

Cheddar Apple Bake

4 slices whole wheat bread
2 Golden Delicious apples, peeled, cored and thinly sliced
¼ cup chopped sweet onion
2 cups shredded Cheddar cheese
2 tablespoons butter or margarine
⅓ cup flour
2 cups milk
2 teaspoons TABASCO® brand Pepper Sauce
½ teaspoon salt
1 egg

Preheat oven to 350°F. Grease 12×8-inch baking dish. Line dish with bread slices, cutting to fit. Top with sliced apples, onion and cheese.

Melt butter in 2-quart saucepan over medium heat. Stir in flour; cook until mixture is bubbly. Stir in milk, TABASCO® Sauce and salt. Heat to boiling; cook until thickened. Remove from heat and cool slightly; whisk in egg. Spoon sauce over cheese in baking dish.

Bake 45 minutes or until puffy and golden. *Makes 6 servings*

Baked Beans with Ham

1 cup chopped onion
2 tablespoons vegetable oil
2 cans (16 ounces each) beans with tomato sauce
1½ cups diced lean ham
6 tablespoons honey
3½ tablespoons prepared mustard
Salt and pepper to taste

Cook and stir onion in oil in large skillet over medium heat until tender. Add remaining ingredients; mix thoroughly. Spoon into 1½-quart baking dish. Bake, covered, at 350°F 45 minutes. Uncover during last 15 minutes of cooking if drier beans are desired. *Makes 6 servings*

Favorite recipe from National Honey Board

Summer Squash Casserole

2 pounds small yellow summer squash, sliced
1 medium onion, sliced
¼ cup water
1 teaspoon salt
1 cup milk
2 large eggs, slightly beaten
3 tablespoons all-purpose flour
3 tablespoons CABOT® Salted Butter, melted, divided
½ teaspoon ground black pepper
2 cups grated CABOT® Sharp Cheddar (about 8 ounces),
divided
¼ cup fresh bread crumbs

1. Preheat oven to 350°F. Butter 1½-quart baking dish or coat with nonstick cooking spray and set aside.

2. In saucepan, bring squash, onion, water and salt to boil. Cover pan and simmer until squash is tender, about 20 minutes.

3. Drain squash and onion thoroughly, then mash. Add milk, eggs, flour, 1 tablespoon melted butter and pepper; mix well.

4. Reserve about 3 tablespoons cheese and mix remaining cheese into squash. Transfer squash to prepared baking dish.

5. Bake for 30 minutes or until knife inserted in center comes out almost clean, about 30 minutes.

6. Meanwhile, toss bread crumbs with remaining melted butter. Sprinkle over casserole, then sprinkle with reserved cheese. Return to oven for about 5 minutes or until crumbs are golden and cheese is melted. *Makes 8 servings*

Potato 'n' Onion Bake

1 pound all-purpose or baking potatoes, thinly sliced
2 medium onions, thinly sliced
2 tablespoons olive oil
½ teaspoon salt
½ teaspoon ground black pepper
2 cups RAGÚ® Chunky Pasta Sauce
3 tablespoons grated Parmesan cheese

Preheat oven to 400°F. In 2-quart baking dish, layer ½ of potatoes, onions, olive oil, salt and pepper; repeat layers. Bake covered 20 minutes or until potatoes are tender. Remove cover; pour Ragú Pasta Sauce over potato mixture; sprinkle with Parmesan cheese. Bake an additional 10 minutes or until heated through.

Makes 4 servings

Broccoli Cheese Casserole

1 can (10¾ ounces) condensed cream of broccoli soup
1 cup milk
½ cup water
1 tablespoon butter or margarine (optional)
1 box UNCLE BEN'S® COUNTRY INN® Broccoli Rice
**   Au Gratin**
1 package (14 to 16 ounces) frozen broccoli florets, thawed
1 cup (4 ounces) shredded pizza cheese blend, divided

1. Preheat oven to 350°F.

2. In medium ovenproof skillet, combine soup, milk, water, butter, rice and contents of seasoning packet. Bring to a boil. Stir in broccoli. Cover; reduce heat and simmer for 20 minutes, stirring occasionally.

3. Remove from heat. Stir in ½ cup cheese. Sprinkle remaining cheese on top; bake 5 minutes or until cheese has melted.   *Makes 4 servings*

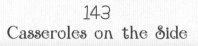
Casseroles on the Side

Mexican Corn Custard Bake

1 can (11 ounces) Mexican-style whole kernel corn, drained
¼ cup all-purpose flour
1 jar (16 ounces) chunky medium salsa, divided
5 eggs, beaten
½ cup sour cream
1⅓ cups *French's*® French Fried Onions, divided
1 cup (4 ounces) shredded Monterey Jack cheese with
**   jalapeño peppers or Cheddar cheese**

Preheat oven to 375°F. Grease 9-inch deep-dish pie plate. Combine corn and flour in large bowl. Stir in ¾ cup salsa, eggs, sour cream and ⅔ *cup* French Fried Onions; mix until well blended. Pour into prepared pie plate. Cover; bake 45 minutes or until custard is set.

Pour remaining salsa around edge of dish. Sprinkle with cheese and remaining ⅔ *cup* onions. Bake, uncovered, 3 minutes or until onions are golden. Cut into wedges to serve.   *Makes 6 servings*

Elegant Ranch Spinach

2 packages (10 ounces each) frozen chopped spinach
¼ pound fresh mushrooms, sliced
¼ cup (½ stick) butter or margarine
2 cups prepared HIDDEN VALLEY® The Original Ranch®
**   Dressing**
½ cup grated Parmesan cheese
1 can (14 ounces) quartered artichoke hearts, drained

Preheat oven to 350°F. Cook spinach according to package directions; drain thoroughly, squeezing out excess liquid. In skillet, sauté mushrooms in butter until softened, about 5 minutes. In large bowl, whisk together salad dressing and cheese; stir in spinach, mushrooms and artichoke hearts. Pour mixture into lightly buttered 2-quart casserole. Cover and bake until heated through, 20 to 30 minutes.

Makes 6 servings

Curried Cauliflower & Cashews

1 medium head cauliflower, broken into florets (about 4 cups)
½ cup water
¾ cup toasted unsalted cashews
3 tablespoons butter, divided
2 tablespoons all-purpose flour
1 tablespoon curry powder
1¼ cups milk
   Salt and black pepper
1 cup dry bread crumbs
   Additional toasted unsalted cashews (optional)
1 jar prepared mango chutney (optional)

1. Preheat oven to 350°F. Grease 2-quart casserole.

2. Place cauliflower in large microwavable dish. Add water. Microwave on HIGH about 4 minutes or until almost tender. Drain and place in prepared casserole. Add ¾ cup cashews; stir until blended.

3. Melt 2 tablespoons butter in medium saucepan. Add flour and curry powder; cook and stir 2 minutes over medium heat. Add milk, whisking constantly; cook and stir until mixture thickens slightly. Season with salt and pepper.

4. Pour sauce over cauliflower mixture; stir to coat evenly. Top with bread crumbs. Dot with remaining 1 tablespoon butter.

5. Bake 45 minutes or until lightly browned. Garnish with additional cashews and serve with chutney. *Makes 8 servings*

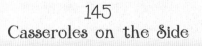

Spinach Pie Side

1⅓ cups *French's®* French Fried Onions, divided
½ cup plain dry bread crumbs
3 tablespoons butter or margarine, melted
1 package (10 ounces) frozen chopped spinach, thawed and
    well drained
3 eggs
½ cup milk
½ cup ricotta cheese
½ teaspoon salt
½ cup (2 ounces) shredded mozzarella cheese

1. Preheat oven to 350°F. In medium bowl, press ⅔ *cup* French Fried Onions with back of spoon until finely crushed. Stir in bread crumbs and butter. Press mixture firmly onto bottom of 9-inch pie plate. Bake 10 minutes; set aside.

2. Combine spinach, eggs, milk, ricotta cheese and salt in large bowl; stir with fork until well blended. Pour into prepared crust. Bake 35 minutes or until tip of knife inserted near center of pie comes out clean.

3. Sprinkle with mozzarella cheese and remaining ⅔ *cup* onions. Bake 5 minutes or until onions are golden. *Makes 6 to 8 servings*

Cheesy Broccoli Bake

1 (10-ounce) package frozen chopped broccoli
1 (10¾-ounce) can condensed Cheddar cheese soup
½ cup sour cream
2 cups (12 ounces) chopped CURE 81® ham
2 cups cooked rice
½ cup soft, torn bread crumbs
1 tablespoon butter or margarine, melted

Heat oven to 350°F. Cook broccoli according to package directions; drain. Combine soup and sour cream. Stir in broccoli, ham and rice. Spoon into 1½-quart casserole. Combine bread crumbs and butter; sprinkle over casserole. Bake 30 to 35 minutes or until thoroughly heated. *Makes 4 to 6 servings*

Mediterranean Vegetable Bake

2 tomatoes, sliced
1 small red onion, sliced
1 medium zucchini, sliced
1 small eggplant, sliced
1 large portobello mushroom, sliced
2 cloves garlic, finely chopped
3 tablespoons olive oil
2 teaspoons chopped fresh rosemary
⅔ cup dry white wine
Salt
Black pepper

1. Preheat oven to 350°F. Grease bottom of oval casserole or 13×9-inch baking dish.

2. Arrange slices of vegetables in rows, alternating different types and overlapping slices in pan to make attractive arrangement. Sprinkle garlic evenly over top. Mix olive oil with rosemary in small bowl; spread over top.

3. Pour wine over vegetables; season with salt and pepper. Loosely cover with foil. Bake 20 minutes. Uncover and bake an additional 10 to 15 minutes or until vegetables are tender.

Makes 4 to 6 servings

Tip: Serve this casserole with crusty bread to soak up the delicious juices. Use whatever vegetables you have on hand or in your garden.

Portobello mushrooms have tough,
woody stems which should be removed
before using the mushrooms in a recipe.

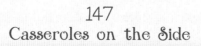

Potato-Turnip Pudding

3 pounds potatoes, peeled
2 pounds turnips, peeled
2 large onions, peeled
½ cup dry bread crumbs
½ cup FILIPPO BERIO® Olive Oil
3 eggs, lightly beaten
1 teaspoon white pepper
½ teaspoon salt
½ teaspoon ground sumac* or paprika

*Sumac can be found in Middle Eastern or specialty food shops.

Preheat oven to 350°F. Grease 13×9-inch pan with olive oil. Shred potatoes, turnips and onions in food processor using grater disk or by hand using metal grater. Discard any liquid that accumulates. (Grated potatoes will discolor quickly. If grating by hand, reserve grated potatoes in bowl of ice water to slow discoloration. Drain well before combining with other ingredients.) In large bowl, combine potatoes, turnips, onions, bread crumbs, olive oil, eggs, pepper, salt and sumac. Spoon into prepared dish. Bake 1 hour or until top is crusty and brown but center is still moist. *Makes 12 to 15 servings*

Hash Brown Bake

1 packet (1 ounce) HIDDEN VALLEY® The Original Ranch®
Salad Dressing & Seasoning Mix
1¼ cups milk
3 ounces cream cheese
6 cups hash browns (frozen shredded potatoes)
1 tablespoon bacon bits
½ cup shredded sharp Cheddar cheese

In blender, combine salad dressing & seasoning mix, milk and cream cheese. Pour over potatoes and bacon bits in 9-inch baking dish. Top with cheese. Bake at 350°F for 35 minutes. *Makes 4 servings*

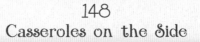

Basque Bean Casserole

1 pound dried beans (Great Northern, yellow eye or pinto)
4½ cups cold water
¼ pound unsliced bacon or salt pork
2 medium leeks, thinly sliced
2 cups chopped onions
1 medium whole onion
6 whole cloves
1 can (13¾ ounces) chicken broth
5 carrots, cut into 1-inch slices
3 cloves garlic, minced
2 teaspoons TABASCO® brand Pepper Sauce
1 teaspoon dried thyme leaves
1 teaspoon dried marjoram leaves
1 teaspoon dried sage leaves
2 bay leaves
6 whole black peppercorns
1 can (16 ounces) whole tomatoes, undrained, crushed
1 pound Polish sausage, cut into 1-inch slices

In 6-quart Dutch oven or saucepan, combine beans and water. Let soak 2 hours. *Do not drain beans.* Meanwhile, in skillet over medium heat, brown bacon on both sides. Remove bacon from skillet. Add leeks and chopped onions. Cook 10 minutes. Add to soaked beans. Stud whole onion with cloves. Add onion, chicken broth, carrots, garlic, TABASCO® Sauce, thyme, marjoram, sage, bay leaves and peppercorns. Bring to a boil. Reduce heat and simmer, covered, 1 hour. Stir in tomatoes and sausage. Cover; bake in preheated 350°F oven 1 hour or until almost all liquid is absorbed.

Makes 6 to 8 servings

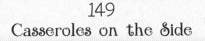

Scalloped Potatoes
with Gorgonzola

1 (14½-ounce) can chicken broth
1½ cups whipping cream
4 teaspoons minced garlic
1½ teaspoons dried sage leaves
1 cup BELGIOIOSO® Gorgonzola Cheese
2¼ pounds russet potatoes, peeled, halved and thinly sliced
Salt and pepper to taste

Preheat oven to 375°F. In heavy saucepan, simmer broth, cream, garlic and sage 5 minutes or until slightly thickened. Add BelGioioso® Gorgonzola Cheese and stir until melted. Remove from heat.

Place potatoes in large bowl and season with salt and pepper. Arrange half of potatoes in 13×9×2-inch glass baking dish. Pour half of cream mixture over top of potatoes. Repeat layers with remaining potatoes and cream mixture. Bake until potatoes are tender, about 1¼ hours. Let stand 15 minutes before serving.   *Makes 8 servings*

Potato & Cauliflower Bake

4 cups frozen country-style hash browns
1 large head cauliflower, cut into small florets (about 4 cups)
2 cups (8 ounces) shredded Cheddar cheese, divided
1 cup chopped onion
¼ cup diced red bell pepper
1¾ cups HIDDEN VALLEY® The Original Ranch® Dressing, divided
½ cup sour cream
½ cup plain dry bread crumbs

Mix hash browns, cauliflower, 1 cup cheese, onion and bell pepper in a large bowl. Whisk 1½ cups dressing and sour cream. Pour over potato mixture; mix well. Transfer to a 2-quart baking dish. Mix remaining 1 cup cheese, ¼ cup dressing and bread crumbs. Sprinkle over casserole. Bake at 350°F for 60 minutes, until browned, bubbly and cauliflower is tender. Let stand for 10 minutes before serving.   *Makes 10 servings*

Indonesian Honey-Baked Beans

2 cans (15 ounces each) white beans, drained
2 apples, peeled and diced
1 small onion, diced
⅔ cup honey
½ cup golden raisins
⅓ cup sweet pickle relish
1 tablespoon prepared mustard
1 teaspoon curry powder or to taste
Salt to taste

Combine all ingredients in 2½-quart casserole. Add enough water just to cover. Bake at 300°F about 1½ hours, adding more water if needed.

Makes 8 servings

Favorite recipe from National Honey Board

Green Bean and Onion Casserole

1 jar (1 pound) RAGÚ® Cheese Creations!® Classic Alfredo Sauce
2 packages (9 ounces each) frozen green beans, thawed
1 can (2.8 ounces) French fried onions, divided
¼ teaspoon ground white pepper
1 tablespoon grated Parmesan cheese (optional)

1. Preheat oven to 350°F. In 1½-quart casserole, combine Ragú Alfredo Sauce, green beans, ½ of onions and pepper; sprinkle with cheese.

2. Bake uncovered 25 minutes or until hot and bubbling. Top with remaining onions and bake an additional 5 minutes.

Makes 6 servings

Prep Time: 5 minutes • Cook Time: 30 minutes

Baked Spanish Rice and Barley

½ cup chopped onion
½ cup chopped green bell pepper
2 cloves garlic, minced
2 teaspoons vegetable oil
1 cup coarsely chopped seeded tomatoes
1 cup chicken broth
½ cup uncooked white rice
½ cup water
3 tablespoons quick-cooking barley
¼ teaspoon black pepper
⅛ teaspoon salt

1. Preheat oven to 350°F. Coat 1½-quart casserole with nonstick cooking spray. Cook and stir onion, bell pepper and garlic in oil in medium saucepan over medium heat until vegetables are tender. Stir in tomatoes, broth, rice, water, barley, black pepper and salt. Bring to a boil over high heat.

2. Pour mixture into prepared casserole. Cover; bake 25 to 30 minutes or until rice and barley are tender and liquid is absorbed. Fluff rice mixture with fork.   *Makes 4 servings*

Festive Potato and Squash Casserole

3 pounds large baking potatoes, pierced with a fork
2 butternut squash (2½ pounds)
1 cup milk
¼ teaspoon ground nutmeg
1 teaspoon dried fines herbes
1¾ cups shredded JARLSBERG cheese, divided
    Salt and freshly ground black pepper to taste

Bake potatoes and squash in 350°F oven until tender, about 1¼ to 1½ hours. (Place foil under squash to prevent drips in oven.)

Casseroles on the Side

Scoop potato pulp into large bowl. Peel and seed squash. Using potato masher or electric beater, mash squash with potatoes, milk, nutmeg and fines herbes.

Stir 1¼ cups cheese into squash mixture; season with salt and pepper. Spoon mixture into shallow 2- or 2½-quart baking dish and sprinkle with remaining ½ cup cheese. Bake at 350°F for 30 to 40 minutes or until heated through and beginning to brown.

Makes 8 to 10 servings

Maple Link Sweet Potatoes and Apples

4 medium to large sweet potatoes
2 Granny Smith or other tart apples
1 (12-ounce) package BOB EVANS® Maple Links
½ teaspoon salt
¾ cup packed brown sugar, divided
¼ teaspoon ground nutmeg
¼ teaspoon ground cinnamon
¼ cup butter or margarine
1 cup apple juice

Cook unpeeled potatoes in 4 quarts boiling water 15 minutes. Drain and cool slightly. Peel and cut into ¼-inch slices. Peel, core and cut apples into ¼-inch slices. Preheat oven to 350°F. Cook sausage in large skillet until browned. Drain off any drippings; place sausage on paper towels. Cut each sausage link into 3 pieces. Arrange potatoes, apples and sausage alternately in buttered 13×9-inch (or similar size) baking dish. Sprinkle with salt, ½ cup brown sugar, nutmeg and cinnamon. Dot with butter. Pour apple juice over top. Cover and bake 30 minutes. Remove from oven; sprinkle with remaining ¼ cup brown sugar. Bake, uncovered, 25 to 30 minutes more or until lightly browned and potatoes are tender. Refrigerate leftovers. *Makes 8 servings*

The publisher would like to thank the companies and organizations listed below for the use of their recipes and photographs in this publication.

Bays English Muffin Corporation

Alouette® Cheese, Chavrie® Cheese, Saladena®

BelGioioso® Cheese, Inc.

Birds Eye Foods

Bob Evans®

Cabot® Creamery Cooperative

Colorado Potato Administrative Committee

Crisco is a registered trademark of The J.M. Smucker Company

Cucina Classica Italiana, Inc.

Del Monte Corporation

Filippo Berio® Olive Oil

The Golden Grain Company®

Guiltless Gourmet®

Heinz North America

The Hidden Valley® Food Products Company

Hillshire Farm®

Holland House® is a registered trademark of Mott's, LLP

Hormel Foods, LLC

Jennie-O Turkey Store®

Lawry's® Foods

Lucini Italia Co.

MASTERFOODS USA

McIlhenny Company (TABASCO® brand Pepper Sauce)

Michigan Apple Committee

Minnesota Cultivated Wild Rice Council

Mrs. Dash®

National Chicken Council / US Poultry & Egg Association

National Fisheries Institute

National Honey Board

National Turkey Federation

Nestlé USA

Newman's Own, Inc.®

Norseland, Inc.

North Dakota Beef Commission

Ortega®, A Division of B&G Foods, Inc.

Perdue Farms Incorporated

Reckitt Benckiser Inc.

Sargento® Foods Inc.

Sonoma® Dried Tomatoes

StarKist Seafood Company

Unilever Foods North America

USA Dry Pea & Lentil Council

Veg•All®

Wisconsin Milk Marketing Board

METRIC CONVERSION CHART

VOLUME MEASUREMENTS (dry)

$^1/_8$ teaspoon = 0.5 mL
$^1/_4$ teaspoon = 1 mL
$^1/_2$ teaspoon = 2 mL
$^3/_4$ teaspoon = 4 mL
1 teaspoon = 5 mL
1 tablespoon = 15 mL
2 tablespoons = 30 mL
$^1/_4$ cup = 60 mL
$^1/_3$ cup = 75 mL
$^1/_2$ cup = 125 mL
$^2/_3$ cup = 150 mL
$^3/_4$ cup = 175 mL
1 cup = 250 mL
2 cups = 1 pint = 500 mL
3 cups = 750 mL
4 cups = 1 quart = 1 L

VOLUME MEASUREMENTS (fluid)

1 fluid ounce (2 tablespoons) = 30 mL
4 fluid ounces ($^1/_2$ cup) = 125 mL
8 fluid ounces (1 cup) = 250 mL
12 fluid ounces (1$^1/_2$ cups) = 375 mL
16 fluid ounces (2 cups) = 500 mL

WEIGHTS (mass)

$^1/_2$ ounce = 15 g
1 ounce = 30 g
3 ounces = 90 g
4 ounces = 120 g
8 ounces = 225 g
10 ounces = 285 g
12 ounces = 360 g
16 ounces = 1 pound = 450 g

DIMENSIONS

$^1/_{16}$ inch = 2 mm
$^1/_8$ inch = 3 mm
$^1/_4$ inch = 6 mm
$^1/_2$ inch = 1.5 cm
$^3/_4$ inch = 2 cm
1 inch = 2.5 cm

OVEN TEMPERATURES

250°F = 120°C
275°F = 140°C
300°F = 150°C
325°F = 160°C
350°F = 180°C
375°F = 190°C
400°F = 200°C
425°F = 220°C
450°F = 230°C

BAKING PAN SIZES

Utensil	Size in Inches/Quarts	Metric Volume	Size in Centimeters
Baking or Cake Pan (square or rectangular)	8×8×2	2 L	20×20×5
	9×9×2	2.5 L	23×23×5
	12×8×2	3 L	30×20×5
	13×9×2	3.5 L	33×23×5
Loaf Pan	8×4×3	1.5 L	20×10×7
	9×5×3	2 L	23×13×7
Round Layer Cake Pan	8×1½	1.2 L	20×4
	9×1½	1.5 L	23×4
Pie Plate	8×1¼	750 mL	20×3
	9×1¼	1 L	23×3
Baking Dish or Casserole	1 quart	1 L	—
	1½ quart	1.5 L	—
	2 quart	2 L	—